ATHEISM

ATHEISM

·

Julian Baggini

A BRIEF
INSIGHT

STERLING

New York / London
www.sterlingpublishing.com

STERLING and the distinctive Sterling logo are registered trademarks of Sterling Publishing Co., Inc.

Library of Congress Cataloging-in-Publication Data

Baggini, Julian.
    Atheism / Julian Baggini.
       p. cm. -- (A brief insight)
    Originally published: Oxford ; New York : Oxford University Press, 2003. With new illustrations.
    Includes bibliographical references and index.
    ISBN 978-1-4027-6882-8
    1. Atheism. I. Title.
    BL2747.3.B245 2009
    211'.8--dc22

                                   2009013950

10 9 8 7 6 5 4 3 2 1

Published by Sterling Publishing Co., Inc.
387 Park Avenue South, New York, NY 10016

Published by arrangement with Oxford University Press, Inc.

Distributed in Canada by Sterling Publishing
c/o Canadian Manda Group, 165 Dufferin Street
Toronto, Ontario, Canada M6K 3H6

Book design and layout: The DesignWorks Group

Please see picture credits on page 177 for image copyright information.

Sterling ISBN 978-1-4027-6882-8

For information about custom editions, special sales, premium and
corporate purchases, please contact Sterling Special Sales
Department at 800-805-5489 or specialsales@sterlingpublishing.com.

Frontispiece: For some atheists, the phenomenon of the sun shining through fog seems symbolic of the light of reason shining through the mist of belief. This striking photograph was taken in 2008 in San Francisco, California.

CONTENTS

•

PREFACE

•

IT HAS BEEN A PLEASURE AND A PRIVILEGE to write this book. In keeping with the ethos of this series I have aimed to keep the book readable and enjoyable, avoiding academic dryness, while at the same time endeavoring to maintain a high standard of intellectual rigor and integrity. It is for others to judge whether I have succeeded.

To avoid scholastic sterility, I have not followed strict academic conventions of referencing and footnotes. Instead, I have listed at the end of the book my main sources along with suggestions for further reading. I hope that these provide sufficient credit to the many writers and thinkers whose ideas have informed this work.

This book is intended for a variety of different readers, including atheists looking for a systematic defense and explanation of their position, agnostics who think that they might be atheists after all, and religious believers who have a sincere desire to understand what atheism is all about. The guiding idea has been to produce a book which atheists will be able to give to their friends by way of explanation for their beliefs, after having used it themselves to help organize their thoughts.

There are many people to thank for their contributions to making this book happen. Primarily, they are Marilyn Mason for her initial suggestion that I might give it a go, Shelly Cox for commissioning it, and Katharine Reeve and Emma Simmons for seeing it through to publication. Marsha Filion deserves special mention for fighting the flab in the penultimate draft. Colleagues in the Humanist Philosophers' Group have also helped enrich my understanding of positive atheism over recent years. I would also like to thank David Nash and Roger Griffin for their advice on reading for the history chapter.

ATHEISM

ONE

What Is Atheism?

•

A Walk on the Dark Side?

WHEN I WAS A CHILD I ATTENDED a Roman Catholic primary school. It would serve the cause of militant atheism well if I could report beatings by nuns and fondlings in the sacristy by randy priests, but neither gaudy tale would be true. On the contrary, I was raised in what could be seen as a gentle, benign religious environment. Neither of my parents were Bible-thumpers and none of my teachers was anything other than kind. I do not feel I bear any deep scars brought on by the mild form of indoctrination practiced there, where beliefs were instilled by constant repetition and reinforcement rather than any overt coercion. Indeed, in

Reverend Ernest James Pace, D.D. (1879–1946), was an artist, a missionary, and a teacher affiliated with the Moody Bible Institute. His book *Christian Cartoons* was published in 1922, and contains many images similar to the one seen here. A figure looking remarkably like Sigmund Freud leads the way into the "darkness" of unbelief.

many ways the power the Church exerted over me was very weak. When I moved to a non-Catholic secondary school I soon moved over to Methodism, and by the time I left school I had given up religious belief altogether. I had become an atheist, a person who believes there is no God or gods.

Yet even this mild form of religious upbringing has had some long-term effects. Back when I was at primary school, the very word "atheist" would conjure up dark images of something sinister, evil, and threatening. Belief in God and obedience to his will was constitutive of our conception of goodness, and therefore any belief that rejected God was by definition opposed to the good. Atheists could only belong to the dark side.

Of course, now I do not subscribe to any of the beliefs that form part of this bleak view of atheism and its dangers. Goodness and belief in God are, to my mind, entirely separate and atheism is, properly understood, a positive world view. Yet when I think of the word "atheist," something of the dark smudge my Catholic mentors smeared over it remains. On an emotional level, they succeeded in forging an

This illustration, created by an unknown artist from Strasbourg, France, around 1419, comes from the *Legenda Aurea*, a hagiography compiled in the thirteenth century. It shows Saint Patrick's purgatory, a pit in the ground that—according to legend—God created to demonstrate the horrors of purgatory to potential converts who wanted proof of God's existence.

association between atheism and the sinister, the negative, and the evil. This stain is now but a residue, hardly noticeable to my conscious mind. But it cannot be entirely removed, and my attention is often involuntarily drawn toward it, as the eye is to a barely perceptible flaw that, once noticed, cannot be forgotten.

My experience could be unusual and in its details perhaps there are few who will hear echoes of their own lives. However, I believe there is one respect in which my experience is not at all unusual. We human beings often claim that it is our ability to think which distinguishes us from other animals. We are *homo sapiens*—thinking hominids—our capacity to reason our distinctive and highest feature. Yet we are not purely rational. It is not just that we are often in the grip of irrational or non-rational forces and desires, it is that our thinking is itself infused with emotion. These feelings shape our thought, often without us realizing it.

The reason I draw attention to this fact is that this book is almost entirely about the rational case for atheism. For this I make no apologies. If we are to make the case for any point of view, the best way to do so is always to appeal to reasons and arguments that can command the widest possible support. However, I am also aware that we do not approach such rational discussions with blank, open minds. We come to them with prejudices, fears, and commitments. Some of these are not founded on reason and that confers on them a certain immunity to the power of rational argumentation. So it is with atheism, on which few readers will have a neutral outlook. It is my guess that many readers, even those who have rejected religion, will have more negative associations for atheism than positive ones.

This is important, because such associations can interfere with clear thinking, leading us to prejudge issues and reject arguments without good

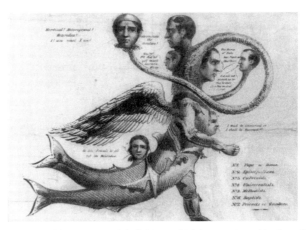

A.M. Bouton created this cartoon entitled *The Mystery of Babylon* in 1835 to satirize the established Christian denominations prevalent in nineteenth-century America. The cartoon's chimera-like beast boasts seven heads, each representing a form of religious belief—or intolerance.

grounds. If you have a deep-rooted image of atheists as miserable, pessimistic amoralists, then rational arguments to the contrary may encounter deep psychological resistance.

The grip such feelings have on us can be strong, and we cannot simply will them away. But we can try to become aware of them and compensate for them. In this book I try to show that atheism is, in several respects, not as people think it is. To allow my case as fair a hearing as possible, I would ask that you try to put aside any dark preconceptions you may have about godlessness and try to judge my arguments on their merits.

Atheism Defined

Atheism is in fact extremely simple to define: it is the belief that there is no God or gods. (Henceforth I shall talk simply of belief in God, but the arguments of this book apply equally to monotheistic and polytheistic beliefs.) However, many people think that atheists believe there is no God *and* no morality; or no God *and* no meaning to life; or again no God *and* no human goodness. As we shall see later, there is nothing to stop atheists believing in morality, a meaning for life, or human goodness. Atheism is only intrinsically negative when it comes to belief about God. It is as capable of a positive view of other aspects of life as any other belief.

This remarkable image was created around 1920 by one William Hope (1863–1933), a controversial British medium and "spirit photographer" who was able to convince his unsuspecting clients that he could capture ghostly images of their deceased loved ones on film. In 1922, Hope was exposed as a fraud, but his work was still defended by many ardent supporters, including Sir Arthur Conan Doyle.

There is one respect, however, in which the negativity of the atheist's belief does extend beyond God's existence. The atheist's rejection of belief in God is usually accompanied by a broader rejection of any supernatural or transcendental reality. For example, an atheist does not usually believe in the existence of immortal souls, life after death, ghosts, or supernatural powers. Although strictly speaking an atheist could believe in any of these things and still remain an atheist, for reasons that will become clearer, the arguments and ideas that sustain atheism tend naturally to rule out other beliefs in the supernatural or transcendental.

Atheism contrasts not only with theism and other forms of belief in God, but also with agnosticism—the suspension of belief or disbelief in God. The agnostic claims we cannot know whether God exists and so the only rational option is to reserve judgment. For the agnostic, both the theist and the atheist go too far, in affirming or denying God's existence respectively—we just don't have sufficient evidence or arguments to justify either position. The question of whether people who have no positive belief in God should be agnostics or atheists is an important one, perhaps as important as the question of whether one should positively believe in God or not, and I will discuss it in more detail in the next chapter.

Atheism, Naturalism, and Physicalism

Another problem with atheism's image as an essentially negative belief system is that many assume atheists are simple physicalists (sometimes called materialists). Crude physicalism asserts that the only things that exist are material objects. A slightly less crude version is that only the objects of the physical sciences—physics, chemistry, and biology—exist. The importance of this alternative formulation is that some of the fundamental forces of physics don't seem to be "material objects" in the everyday sense of the word, yet a physicalist would not deny that they exist.

Most atheists are physicalists only in one rather general sense. That is to say, their atheism is motivated at least in part by their naturalism, a belief that there is only the natural world and not any supernatural one. We should call this "naturalism-with-a-small-n" to distinguish it from certain versions of philosophical Naturalism which may make stronger and more specific claims. It will be my claim that this form of naturalism lies at the core of atheism.

This kind of naturalism fits comfortably with a form of physicalism which combines the naturalist claims about the world with the further claim that this world is essentially physical in nature. However, since physicalism does require this further claim it cannot be assumed that naturalist atheists must also be physicalists. Even when they are, we have to understand that the phrase "essentially physical in nature" can be understood in various ways with very different implications.

The Roman poet and philosopher Lucretius (Titus Lucretius Carus, ca. 95–55 BCE) was the author of *De Rerum Natura* (*On the Nature of Things*), a landmark study—in verse—of the material nature of the universe. Lucretius is considered one of the fathers of naturalism, an important philosophical underpinning of atheism.

One way of understanding this claim is to say that it is about substances: the "stuff" out of which all things are made. This brand of physicalism asserts that the only kind of stuff is physical stuff: there are no

Thomas Hobbes (1588–1679) represents an important branch of the materialist tradition in philosophy. When, in 1666, the British House of Commons introduced a bill against atheism and "profaneness," it cited in particular Hobbes's work *Leviathan*. This portrait was painted by the artist William Dobson (1610–46).

nonphysical souls, spirits, or ideas. This is a version of physicalism that many, probably most, atheists can sign up to.

However, there is a stronger view, called eliminative materialism. On this view, not only is it true that the only kind of stuff is physical stuff, it is also true that anything that isn't physical stuff doesn't really exist. So, for example, there is no such thing as a thought or an idea. Eliminative materialism is hard to swallow because it requires us to deny the existence of many things it seems we must believe in. How, for instance, are we to deny that minds exist when the fact that we have minds ourselves seems to be such a central feature of our very existence?

Many critics of atheism seem to assume that atheists are physicalists (as a matter of fact mostly true) and that physicalism is the same as eliminative materialism (logically false). They therefore use the apparent absurdity of eliminative materialism as a *reductio ad absurdum* of atheist belief. Put crudely, the atheist is portrayed as a kind of nihilist, who not only denies the existence of God, but also denies the existence of anything other than physical objects. Such an impoverished existence has little to recommend it.

But physicalism does not necessarily entail eliminative materialism. All physicalism says is that the only kind of stuff is physical stuff. That does not mean, for example, that minds do not exist. All it means is that minds, whatever they are, are not lumps of stuff. To think that they are is to make what Gilbert Ryle termed a "category mistake." The mistake is to think of mind and matter as two different varieties of the one category, "stuff." That is false. In my head there are not two different kinds of stuff—mental (my mind) and physical (my brain)—which somehow work alongside one other. Rather, for the physicalist, there is only one lump of stuff in my head, which is my brain. It is true, in one very important sense, to say I have a mind, in that I am capable of thought or consciousness. However, I make a mistake if I think that the statement "I have a mind" entails that "I am in part constituted by a mental, nonmaterial substance."

The British philosopher and professor Gilbert Ryle (1900–1976) appears here at a joint meeting of the Aristotelian Society and the Mind Association at Birmingham University in England, held in August of 1952. Ryle believed that the workings of the mind are not distinct from the actions of the body.

If this seems a little difficult to get a grip on, just consider love. No one thinks that love is a special kind of substance—that there is physical stuff and love-stuff. Nor does anyone think that love is some kind of physical object. Yet many people believe in love, feel love, give love, and so on. Love is real but it is not a substance. If we have no problem with this thought, why do we have a problem with the idea that minds are real but are not a special kind of mental substance? Many things are real that are not things in the sense of being lumps of stuff, and there is no great metaphysical mystery about that.

These are philosophically deep waters which we can but dip our toes into here. For the moment, I just want to stress that the atheist is not a crude denier of all that is not physical, if by "physical" we mean a physical substance. What most atheists do believe is that although there is only one kind of stuff in the universe and it is physical, out of this stuff come minds, beauty, emotions, moral values—in short, the full gamut of phenomena that gives richness to human life.

It should be remembered that most atheism is rooted not in the specific claims of physicalism but the broader claims of naturalism. All we need to remember is that the natural world is home to consciousness, emotion, and beauty and not just atoms and fundamental physical forces. Once more, the moral of the story is that the atheist denies the existence of God, but is not by nature a denier period.

A Positive Case for Atheism

My main aim in this book is to provide a positive case for atheism, one that is not simply about rubbishing religious belief. In other words, I hope it will be as much about why one should be an atheist as why one should *not* be a theist. Many critics of atheism will say that this is not possible, since atheism is parasitic on religion. This is evident in its very name—atheism is a-theism: the negation of theistic belief. Hence atheism is by its very nature negative and relies for its existence on the religious beliefs it rejects.

I think this view is profoundly mistaken. Its initial plausibility is based on a very crude piece of flawed reasoning we can call the etymological fallacy. This is the mistake of thinking that one can best understand what a word means by understanding its origin. But this is evidently not always true. For example, the etymology of "philosophy" is the Greek for "love of wisdom." Yet one cannot really understand what philosophy means today simply by knowing this etymological fact. Likewise, if you go into an Italian restaurant knowing only that "tagliatelle" literally means "little boot laces," you won't have much idea what you're going to end up eating if you order it. So the mere fact that the word "atheist" is constructed as a negation of theism is not enough to show that it is essentially negative.

They *look* like boot laces, but they're not—they're tagliatelle, pasta noodles in the shape of boot laces. The etymological fallacy states that we can best understand a word's meaning by examining its origin, a practice that doesn't work in the case of atheism (or orecchiette or conchiglie, either).

Etymology aside, we can see how casting atheism in a negative light is no more than a historical accident. Consider this story, which begins as fact and ends as fiction.

In Scotland there is a deep lake called Loch Ness. Many people in Scotland—almost certainly the majority—believe that the lake is like other lochs in the country. Their beliefs about the lake are what we might call normal. But that is not to say they have no particular beliefs. It's just that the beliefs they have are so ordinary that they do not require elucidation. They believe that the lake is a natural phenomenon of a certain size, that certain fish live in it, and so on.

However, some people believe that the loch contains a strange creature, known as the Loch Ness Monster. Many claim to have seen it, although no firm evidence of its existence has ever been presented. So far our story is simple fact. Now imagine how the story could develop.

The number of believers in the monster starts to grow. Soon, a word is coined to describe them: they are part-mockingly called "Nessies." (Many names of religions started as mocking nicknames: Methodist, Quaker, and even Christian all started out this way.) However, the number of Nessies continues to increase and the name ceases to become a joke. Despite the fact that the evidence for the monster's existence is still lacking, soon being a Nessie is the norm and it is the people previously thought of as normal who are in the minority. They soon get their own name, "Anessies"—those who don't believe in the monster.

The dark clouds looming over Loch Ness, near Inverness, Scotland, seem appropriate to its legendary reputation as home of the Loch Ness Monster. The ruins of Urquhart Castle, seen in the foreground, date from the thirteenth century. It is near the castle that the majority of "Nessie" sightings occur. The castle is the third-busiest site run by Historic Scotland, and visitors no doubt comprise theists and atheists, Nessies and Anessies.

Is it true to say that the beliefs of Anessies are parasitic on those of the Nessies? That can't be true, because the Anessies' beliefs predate those of the Nessies. The key point is not one of chronology, however. The key is that the Anessies would believe exactly the same as they do now even if Nessies had never existed. What the rise of the Nessies did was to give a name to a set of beliefs that had always existed but which was considered so unexceptional that it required no special label.

The moral of the story should be clear. Atheists subscribe to a certain world view that includes numerous beliefs about the world and what is in it. Theists say that there is something else that also exists—God. If theists did not exist, atheists still would, but perhaps there would be no special

This photograph of a creature that some claim to be the Loch Ness Monster, taken on April 19, 1934, is one of two pictures known as the "surgeon's photographs." It was allegedly taken by Colonel Robert Kenneth Wilson, though it was later exposed as a hoax by a man named Chris Spurling, who, on his deathbed, revealed that he staged the pictures with the help of his stepfather, Marmaduke Wetherell; his stepbrother, Ian Wetherell; and Wilson. References to a monster in Loch Ness date back to the *Vita Columbae*, a seventh-century biography of Saint Columba.

name for them. But since theism has become so dominant in our world, with so many people believing in God or gods, atheism has come to be defined in contrast to theism. That makes it no more parasitic on religion than the beliefs of the Anessies are parasitic on those of the Nessies.

The absurdity of saying that atheism is parasitic on religious belief is perhaps made most clear by considering what would happen if everyone ceased to believe in God. If atheism were parasitic on religion, then surely it could not exist without religion. But in this imagined scenario, what we would have would not be the end of atheism but its triumph. Atheism no more needs religion than atheists do.

Honk If You're an Atheist

In summary, the aim of this book is to provide a positive view of atheism, one which does not make the mistake of thinking that atheism can only exist as a parasitic rival to theism, or that atheism is essentially negative about a whole range of beliefs other than those concerning God's existence. Atheism is not essentially negative in either of these senses. Atheists can be indifferent rather than hostile to religious belief. They can be more sensitive to aesthetic experience, more moral, or more attuned to natural beauty than many theists. There is no more reason for them to be pessimistic or depressive than there is for the religious to be so.

However, I would not want to fall into the trap of trying so hard to correct preconceptions that I end up painting an unduly rosy picture of atheism. Most atheists see themselves as realists—their atheism is a part of their willingness to square up to the world as it is and face it without recourse to superstition or comforting fictions about a life to come or a benevolent power looking after us. Being such realists requires us to accept that much of what goes on in this world is unpleasant. Bad things happen, people have miserable lives, and you never know when blind luck (not fate) might intervene to change your own life, for the better or for the worse.

Because of this, atheists tend to find relentless, blind cheeriness anathema. There is a bleak humor for the atheist in evangelical Christians with their bumper stickers asking you to "honk if you love Jesus." What is both comic and depressing about the sticker is that it reflects the cheering self-assuredness of believers who need only remind themselves of their religious belief to feel that little bit better about the world. The crass simplicity of this world view can be darkly comic, in that it throws into relief how easy it is for humans to give in to comforting idiocy.

Happy-clappy atheism is just as objectionable, but fortunately atheism's inherent realism provides, on the whole, a kind of immunity to it. That's why you won't see a "honk if you're an atheist" bumper sticker, at least not an unironic one. However, when seeking to overturn the negative caricature of atheism that is so prevalent, it is tempting to overemphasize how positive it can be. The truth is that there is no *a priori* link between being an atheist and having a positive or negative outlook. In arguing that atheism need not be negative and can be positive, I am not claiming that becoming an atheist is a passport to happiness. Fulfillment in this life is harder work than that, and it is a mark of atheism's realism and optimism that an acceptance of this sober truth still leaves fulfillment within our reach.

The license plate on this car afflicted by the ravages of Hurricane Katrina in New Orleans illustrates an unfortunate—but sometimes, to atheists, darkly comic—faith in the unknown. The photograph was taken in early 2006, several months after the August 2005 hurricane, in the city's formerly flooded Eighth Ward neighborhood.

TWO

The Case for Atheism

●

How to Make a Case for Anything

IN THIS CHAPTER I SET OUT to make a case for atheism. Before I do so, however, I want to say a few words about the whole business of making a case for any particular point of view. This is needed because unless we have some kind of idea about what in general makes a good case for something we have little chance of assessing any particular case.

In the broadest possible terms, one can make a case by a combination of argument, evidence, and rhetoric. Arguments can be good or bad and come in various varieties, as we shall shortly see. Evidence too can be strong or weak. Rhetoric is here the odd man out because good rhetoric

Rhetoric—traditionally identified as one of the seven liberal arts, along with grammar, logic, arithmetic, music, geometry, and astronomy—is one of the tools a person can use to make a persuasive case for a given point of view, including atheism. This allegorical figure of Rhetoric is part of a larger work by the painter Giuseppe Cesari (1568–1640).

does not make a better case, it merely makes it more persuasive. Rhetoric is simply the use of language to persuade, and it can be used to persuade us of falsehoods as well as truths.

Religious preachers and politicians have traditionally been good at rhetoric. Jesus, for instance, is reputed to have said "He who is not with me is against me" (Matthew, 12:30), a rhetorical ploy picked up by George W. Bush two thousand years later when he declared countries were either "with us or with the terrorists." This is pure rhetoric because, although potentially persuasive, it has no basis in fact or logic. It is simply not true that a person who is not for Bush or Jesus must be against them. One can be undecided, or not convinced enough to give them full support but sympathetic enough not to turn against them. But in making the choice seem stark, Bush and Jesus both hoped to persuade people to come off the fence and back them: "Well I'm not against them, so therefore I should really just come out and support them."

In what follows I want to avoid pure rhetoric and expose it when it is used against atheism. But for the most part I want to focus on the genuine components of a good case for atheism: evidence and argument.

Evidence

In ordinary speech we appeal to all kinds of evidence: "I heard it on the news"; "I saw it with my own eyes"; "In tests eight out of ten cats said their owners preferred it."

The problem is, of course, that not all evidence is good evidence. What makes good evidence is a big issue, but the key general principle is that evidence is stronger if it is available to inspection by more people on repeated occasions; and worse if it is confined to the testimony of a small number of people on limited occasions. We can see how this

principle works by considering two extreme examples. The evidence that water freezes at zero degrees centigrade is an example of the best kind of evidence. In principle, anyone can test this out at any time for themselves and each test makes the evidence more compelling.

Now consider the other extreme, often called anecdotal evidence because it relies upon the testimony of a single person relating one incident. Someone claims that they saw their dog spontaneously combust right before their very eyes. Is this good evidence for the existence of spontaneous canine combustion? Not at all, for various reasons. First, as the Scottish philosopher David Hume pointed out, the evidence has to be balanced against the

Proof that water freezes at zero degrees centigrade isn't hard to find. This thermometer is easily available for repeated inspection by large numbers of people, which increases its value as evidence.

much larger amount of evidence that dogs don't just burst into flames. Hume's point is not that the testimony of this one person isn't evidence at all. It is rather that it is insignificant when we compare it to all the other evidence we have that spontaneous canine combustion does not take place.

David Hume (1711–76), seen here in this 1766 portrait by Allan Ramsay, was one of the first philosophers of the modern era to propound a thoroughly naturalistic philosophy, one that rejected the then-prevalent idea that human minds are essentially miniature versions of the divine mind. Hume's philosophy relied instead on human reason to achieve insight into reality.

A second reason why it is not good evidence is that, sadly, human beings are not very good at interpreting their experiences, especially unusual ones. Take as a simple example the experience of seeing an illusionist who pretends to have real powers bending a metal spoon without apparently exerting any physical force. You will hear people persuaded by such experiments say that they "saw the person bend the spoon with their thoughts." Of course they saw no such thing, not least because they could not see the illusionist's thoughts, which means they couldn't have seen the thoughts bend the metal. What they saw was a spoon bend, while they did not see any physical force being exerted upon it, that's all. Everything else is interpretation.

To say this is not to call the witness a liar or a fool. They are neither. They did not lie, they were just mistaken, and they are not fools but victims of clever tricksters.

We can see how the merits of these two extremes of evidence compare by considering how we show anecdotal evidence to be weak. In the case of spontaneous canine combustion, the failure of the episode to ever be repeated is one reason why we take the anecdotal evidence for its occurrence to be weak. If dogs did burst into flames for no apparent reason quite regularly, then the evidence would be stronger: stronger because it is available to inspection by more people on repeated occasions.

We can be similarly skeptical about the strength of evidence for spoon-bending because when the "powers" of the spoon-bender are tested in a situation in which the phenomenon can be observed in laboratory conditions, no such powers are displayed. Again, it seems that the evidence is such that it is not open to the kind of ordinary inspection that the freezing of water is.

Renowned spoon-bending entertainer Uri Geller of Israel poses with a spoon he bent on November 28, 2005, in Geneva, Switzerland. Geller's art confounds the eye, but cannot be verified under laboratory conditions.

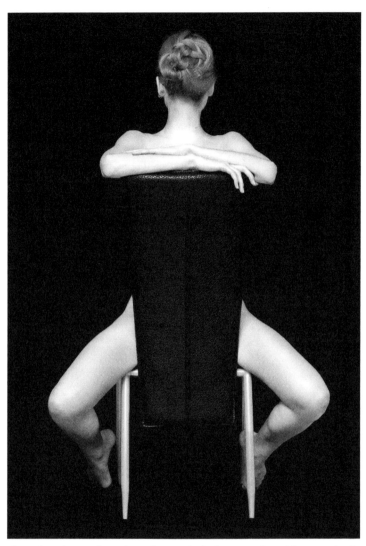

This striking photograph provides another example of a phenomenon that can't be re-created under laboratory conditions, yet still falls under the category of visual evidence, illusory though it may be.

What I want to suggest is that all the strong evidence tells in favor of atheism, and only weak evidence tells against it. In any ordinary case, this would be enough to establish that atheism is true. The situation is comparable to that of water freezing at zero degrees centigrade: all the strong evidence suggests it does. Only the weak evidence of anecdote, myth, hearsay, and illusionists tells against it.

Absence and Evidence

If we fall into the error of seeing atheism purely as an opposition to theism, we might think that the evidence for atheism comprises the evidence against the existence of God. However, as we saw in Chapter 1, atheism is essentially a form of naturalism and so its main evidential base is the evidence for naturalism. This is only evidence against God's existence in a negative sense: that is to say, evidence for God's existence will be found to be lacking and so we will be left with no reason to suppose he exists.

This kind of argument does not satisfy many people who appeal to the principle that "absence of evidence is not evidence of absence." Things are not quite as simple, however, as this slogan makes out. Consider the simple question of whether there is any butter in my fridge. If we don't open the door and have a look inside, there will be an absence of evidence for the butter being there, but this would not add up to evidence of its absence. If we look inside the fridge, thoroughly examine it, and don't find any butter, then we have an absence of evidence which really does add up to evidence of absence. Indeed, it is hard to see what other evidence there could be for something *not* being there other than the failure to find any evidence that it *is* there. Something which does not exist leaves no mark, so it can only be an absence of marks of its existence that can provide evidence for its nonexistence.

The difference between the absence of evidence when we don't look in the fridge and the absence once we have looked is simple: the former is an absence due to a failure to look where evidence might be found; the latter is an absence due to a failure to find evidence where it would be found, if the thing being looked for actually existed. The latter kind of absence of evidence really is strong evidence for absence.

Think about it: the strongest evidence that, for example, there is no elephant in your fridge is that you find no signs of one when you open the fridge door.

So the evidence for atheism is to be found in the fact that there is a plethora of evidence for the truth of naturalism and an absence of evidence for anything else. "Anything else" of course includes God, but it also includes goblins, hobbits, and truly everlasting gobstoppers. There is nothing special about God in this sense. God is just one of the things that atheists don't believe in, it just happens to be the thing that, for historical reasons, gave them their name.

According to most atheists, there is no evidence for the existence of extrasensory perception, despite attempts at verification like the one shown here. In October of 1961, twelve-year-old twins Terry Young (at the table) and Sherry Young (in the foreground), of Jackson, Mississippi, tried to prove their claim that they have the ability to convey their thoughts to each other. Terry is trying to "tell" her sister what card she's holding. Ophelia Rivers, a Mississippi State University psychologist (left), said she was "delighted and convinced" by the girls' performance.

Evidence for Atheism

We are now in a position to look at what the evidence for naturalism, and hence for atheism, is. The claim I would make is that all the strong evidence points to the truth of atheism and only weak evidence counts against it. This may seem like a strong claim but I really do think it is justified.

Consider one of the biggest questions where the evidence has something to contribute: the nature of persons. The atheist's naturalism consists in the view that a human being is a biological animal rather than some kind of embodied spiritual soul, as many religious believers think. This is really rather a minimal claim which offers several alternative ways forward. For instance, some claim that humans are just animals like any other and that humans are not in any sense special or different from other beasts. Others, however, while believing that humans are biological animals, claim that our capacities for consciousness and rational thought make us essentially different from other animals. This idea of "human exceptionalism" has traditionally been a strong thread in atheist humanism.

The point here is not to resolve the dispute, but merely to say that both atheist exceptionalists and their atheist critics are united in the view that, whatever people are, they are first and foremost mortal creatures who do not have immortal, spiritual souls. What is the evidence for this claim? Consider the strong evidence first. The strong evidence about humans all points to their biological nature. For example, consciousness remains in many ways a mystery. But all we do know about it with any certainty points to the fact that it is a product of brain activity and that with no brain, there is no consciousness. In fact, this is so startlingly obvious that it is astonishing that anyone can really doubt it. The data of neurology show that all the diverse experiences which we associate with consciousness correlate with particular patterns of brain activity.

The key word here is, of course, "correlate." To say brain events and conscious experiences correlate is only to say that one always accompanies the other. That is not to say one causes the other. Night follows day, for instance, but it is not caused by day. But while it is true that a correlation does not necessarily indicate a cause, in the case of brains and consciousness the link is at least one of dependency. That is to say, if you inhibit or damage an area of the brain that is correlated with

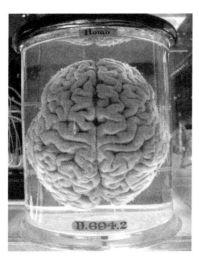

The one and only vessel of consciousness recognized by atheists: the brain.

a particular form of conscious activity, that conscious activity will cease. (More bizarrely, if you stimulate certain areas of the brain you can sometimes induce involuntary conscious activity. For instance, by stimulating the area of the brain associated with humor, you can make someone find anything hilarious.) And although we cannot look into the minds of others, when their brains cease functioning they certainly stop displaying all the signs of conscious life.

If any one thing distinguishes us as individual persons then that must be our capacity for consciousness and rational thought. And if this capacity is entirely dependent on our organic brains, as the strong evidence suggests, then the atheist view that we are mortal, biological organisms is well supported.

For many atheists, that particular issue can be considered settled here, since the evidence is just so overwhelming that we are the mortal creatures they claim. But non-atheists are likely at this point to make two counterobjections. One is to claim that atheists are too sure of themselves, since there is much they simply cannot know about consciousness and its dependency on brains. The other is to point to supposed counterevidence.

If we consider the counterevidence first we will find that it is all of the extremely weak variety. If we were to make a list of the evidence that consciousness can continue beyond the death of the brain, we would have to include evidence such as the testimony of mediums, supposed appearances of ghosts, and near-death experiences. There really isn't any stronger evidence since no dead person has ever been able to communicate with the living so freely as to present good evidence that they exist.

All these forms of evidence are extremely weak. Mediums are unreliable. It is true that some individuals are convinced that they have been contacted by loved ones via mediums. However, such personal convictions cannot make for good evidence. People have many deep emotional needs that can contribute to a willingness to believe which in normal circumstances might be considered gullibility, but in the case of bereavement really deserves a more sympathetic name. And the fact is that no medium has ever been able to tell us something that proves beyond reasonable doubt that he or she is party to information from the "spirit world." Ghosts are even less convincing, and near-death experiences also fail to provide any good evidence that we can survive death. Even their name—*near-death* experiences—points to that.

The non-atheist at this point is likely to retort with a number of pieces of evidence to which they think the atheist cannot reply. What about the medium who led people to the body of a murdered child, information no one living could possibly have? Why do the police use mediums if they are unreliable? How do you explain how the medium told the widow something only her dead husband could possibly have known?

In demanding that the atheist provide a case-by-case rebuttal of all alleged evidence for life after death, the non-atheist is making an unfair demand. It is just impossible for anyone to assess all the individual claims that are made. But the pattern of the atheist's justification

Perhaps no image has conveyed so effectively the absurdity of a séance as this still from the 1922 German silent film *Dr. Mabuse, der Spieler* (*Dr. Mabuse, the Gambler*), directed by Fritz Lang and starring Rudolf Klein-Rogge.

does not require this bit-by-bit demolition. Rather, they can respond by appeal to general principles.

The first general point that should be made is that, on closer inspection, almost all of these alleged pieces of evidence turn out to be much weaker than they are. As David Hume pointed out, we have a natural tendency to be bewitched by wonder and mystery, which gives us a strong desire to believe tales of the extraordinary. The atheist can justly say that, when in all the instances into which they do look further they find the evidence not as it at first seems, they are justified in assuming all similar cases to be equally weak unless proven otherwise. Hence the onus is on

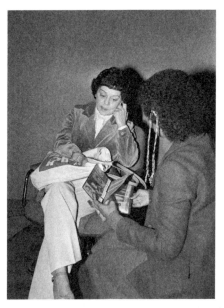

Skeptics of psychic ability claim that some supposed clairvoyants engaged in police work use a technique called retrofitting, in which they mention certain clues and perceptions—like a specific number, or the presence of water at a crime scene—that have a strong likelihood of being true. In this 1980 photograph, the late New Jersey psychic Dorothy Allison (1925–99) talks to an interviewer about the series of child murders that took place in Atlanta between 1979 and 1981. Allison was brought to the city in an unsuccessful attempt to help police solve the case.

the non-atheist, not to demand an explanation from the atheist, but to make a case that is more than just a repetition of hearsay.

But the second response is even more important. All the evidence for life after death that is presented is of the weak variety. None of these so-called cases of communication with the dead has left us with anything approaching the kind of generally observable, verifiable data that is characteristic of strong evidence. So the question for non-atheists must be, why do they think that a few pieces of such weak evidence for life after death will suffice to outweigh the mountain of strong evidence for the mortality of human consciousness? If the evidence for life after death were of the strong variety, its relative rareness might not matter. If, for instance, a person were to stand before a room of people, kill and burn themselves, and then continue to talk and be talked back to, then and afterward, that single survival of death alone would be enough to make atheists reconsider their belief in human mortality. But none of the evidence for life after death even approaches this strength. It smacks of wishful thinking and self-delusion when people are prepared to place more importance on anecdotal weak evidence than they are on strong evidence for our mortality.

This is why even the rare examples of genuinely puzzling evidence for life after death do not clinch it for the non-atheists. Let us say that in one instance (or maybe even a dozen), a medium has said something only the dead could know. The point is still that such rare, unrepeatable pieces of weak evidence are outweighed by the mass of strong evidence for the mortality of the self. Remember that every day millions of reports are made by

Many people who have so-called near-death experiences claim an unusual type of vision during the event—an image of a long tunnel, at the end of which glows a bright light. Often, a human or divine figure stands in the light. To an atheist, these experiences do not constitute evidence of life after death.

mediums. By pure luck alone a few are bound to be uncanny. It would be foolish to consider individual examples of such "communications" greater evidence than all we know about human mortality.

In writing this section I have a strong feeling that my arguments are powerless in the face of a strong desire for belief in life after death. This returns us to the point about absence of evidence and evidence of absence. Just as persons with an obsessive-compulsive disorder can never be sure they have actually locked the door no matter how many times they go back to check, so the person who thinks there may be life after death can never be sure that the possibility has been ruled out for good, no matter how many times the evidence is reviewed. The logical possibility always remains that the piece of "killer evidence" will emerge, the strong, verifiable evidence that we are not mortal after all. This permanent possibility sustains hope and belief in those who want to believe in life after death.

The problem is that such permanent possibilities exist for many beliefs. It is possible, for instance, that tomorrow it will be revealed that you have lived all your life in a virtual reality machine; that aliens have been preparing for an invasion of Earth for the last hundred years; that the pope is a robot; that the Apollo mission never made it to the moon and the whole landing was filmed in a studio; that the evangelical Christians were right all along and Judgment Day has arrived. But the mere possibility that such things might be true is no reason to believe them. Indeed, the fact that the evidence to date suggests strongly they are not true is good reason to disbelieve them.

This is why the claim that atheists overstep the mark in their disbelief is unjustified. People say that, since atheists can never know for sure that there is no life after death, for example, it is foolish for them to not believe in it. At best they should suspend belief and be agnostic. (It is also interesting to note that many of the people who claim that atheists should be agnostics are themselves religious believers. Surely if they were consistent they should become agnostics themselves?)

But this policy would be reckless, since to apply it consistently you would also have to be agnostic about any issue on which there was a possibility that you could be wrong, because there is no absolute certainty and it is possible that evidence might arise to show you are wrong. But who seriously claims we should say "I neither believe nor disbelieve that the pope is a robot," or "As to whether or not eating this piece of chocolate will turn me into an elephant I am completely agnostic." In the absence of any good reasons to believe these outlandish claims, we rightly disbelieve them, we don't just suspend judgment.

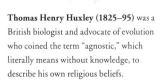

Thomas Henry Huxley (1825–95) was a British biologist and advocate of evolution who coined the term "agnostic," which literally means without knowledge, to describe his own religious beliefs.

Atheism and Dogmatism

Many of those who claim atheists should be agnostics are guilty, I think, of confusing what I will call "firmly held belief" with dogmatism. At the heart of the distinction between the two is the technical term "defeasibility." Beliefs or truth claims are said to be defeasible when the possibility remains open that they could be shown to be wrong. Beliefs or truth claims that are indefeasible are hence ones for which there is no possibility of their being shown to be wrong.

Where to draw the boundary between the defeasible and the indefeasible is a thorny philosophical issue. Traditionally, so-called analytic truths, such as the fact that 1 + 1 = 2 and that all bachelors are unmarried men—statements which appear to be true just by virtue of what they mean—have been thought to be indefeasible, while factual claims about the nature of the world have generally been held to be defeasible. Hence it is possible, however unlikely, that the sun won't rise tomorrow (so the belief that it will is defeasible), but nothing can make 1 + 1 not equal 2 (so the belief that they do is indefeasible). However, several philosophers, notably W. V. O. Quine, have held that even basic truths of mathematics are defeasible. We can't rule out the possibility that we might find reasons to say that 1 + 1 does not always equal 2.

Fortunately, we do not need to enter these deeps waters here. All we need do is borrow the idea of defeasibility to explain the difference between dogmatism and firmly held belief. To be dogmatic is basically to hold that one's beliefs are indefeasible when such a refusal to countenance the possibility of being wrong is not justified. A dogmatic atheist is therefore someone who believes that God does not exist and that there is no way that they could possibly be wrong to hold that belief. A dogmatic theist is similarly someone who believes that God exists and that there is no way that they could possibly be wrong to hold that belief. It would be fair to object to both these dogmatists that their beliefs are unjustified, since there is no way either can be so sure that they are right.

In his 1949 speech *Am I an Atheist or an Agnostic?* the British philosopher Bertrand Russell (1872–1970) described his position: "To my mind the essential thing is that one should base one's arguments upon the kind of grounds that are accepted in science, and one should not regard anything that one accepts as quite certain, but only as probable in a greater or a less degree."

But this does not mean that they should become agnostics. All it means is that they should allow for the defeasibility of their beliefs: they just need to admit it is possible that they could be wrong. This is not agnosticism. Indeed, one can have very strongly held beliefs and still admit their defeasibility. For instance, atheists who say that they believe there are no good reasons for being anything other than an atheist and that they themselves cannot imagine a situation arising in which they would give up their beliefs are still not being dogmatic, just as long as they acknowledge the possibility that they could be wrong. Of course, one is not truly undogmatic unless one sincerely acknowledges this possibility and doesn't just gesture toward it. As long as that sincerity is there, there is no reason why one cannot have firmly held atheist beliefs and thus follow the middle path between unwarranted agnosticism and dogmatism.

Why is this middle path so often missed? I think it is part of a collective myth, which owes its origins to philosophers such as Plato, that knowledge is either absolutely certain or it is not knowledge at all. We tend to think that the mere introduction of grounds for doubt is enough to warrant the suspension of our beliefs. If you can't be sure, don't have an opinion. But this maxim cannot be followed. We cannot be absolutely sure of anything, save perhaps for the fact of our own existence (and even then only at the time we are aware of it). So if we are not justified in believing anything we are not sure of, we would have to suspend belief about everything. This is not the right moral to draw from the truism that absolute certainty is elusive. It does not follow from the fact that we could be wrong that we have no good reasons to think we are right.

I am as opposed to dogmatic atheism as anyone, and I am also opposed to dogmatic theism. Indeed, it is my personal view that dogmatic views of any kind are in general more dangerous than the views themselves. Intelligent atheists often have much more in common with undogmatic theists than one might suppose.

Arguments to the Best Explanation

So far I have argued that atheism is the view best supported by the evidence of experience and that the fact that such conclusive evidence is not watertight is grounds only for rejecting dogmatic belief, not suspending belief altogether and embracing agnosticism.

Because this might still strike some people as too weak an argument, it is worth spending a little time explaining why it is, in fact, the kind of argument best suited to the question in hand. To do this we need to think about how we reason concerning any matters of fact.

The main method we have for doing this is called induction. This is when we argue from what has been observed in the past or present to reach conclusions about what hasn't been observed, in the past, present, or future. Such arguments are premised on the uniformity of nature—

the idea that the laws of nature do not suddenly suspend themselves or change. Note that this is not the same as saying that nature is always predictable. That would be a foolish claim. Many events in nature are extremely unpredictable. But none of this unpredictable behavior breaks natural laws. Freak weather is not uncaused weather.

We all of us make this assumption about the uniformity of nature, every minute of the day. Even if you are just sitting down doing nothing, you relax in the assumptions that gravity is not about to stop keeping you sitting down, that the material the chair is made of will not suddenly turn to liquid, and that the tea you're drinking won't suddenly poison you. But our reliance on the principle is not supported by strict logic. From the premise "This is how things have always been when observed" it does not logically follow that "This is how things always have been, are, and will be." Hence the child who believes their toys come to life when they go to sleep but never when they awake is not making a *logical* error: no truths about what they observe when they are awake can ever provide enough evidence for a logical proof that the same happens while they are asleep.

Nevertheless, we believe the child is mistaken and the reason we do so is that we come to realize that we depend entirely on inductive forms of argument to make sense of the world around us. Atheists can argue that, if we apply this inductive method consistently, their own case is further supported. The evidence of experience is that we live in a world governed by natural laws, that everything that happens in it is explained by natural phenomena. It is true that some things remain unexplained, but the atheist can argue that when an explanation finally does come along for what is unexplained, that explanation is always naturalistic. Experience shows us that to be explained just is to be explained in naturalistic terms. The class of unexplained phenomena therefore is unlikely to contain anything that will come to be explained by anything supernatural.

Induction therefore supports atheists because it is a method of argument we all rely upon, whether we are atheists or religious believers. So it is not an option for non-atheists to reject the admissibility of induction. However, once we accept the inductive method, we should, to be consistent, also accept that it points toward a naturalism that supports atheism, not any kind of supernaturalism that supports theism. And the fact that inductive arguments do not give us absolute certainty is a brute fact we have to live with, since we have to live with the uncertainty of induction to function in the world at all, even just to take a seat.

There is a second type of argument which is based on evidence but which does not admit of strict proof, and this is even more important for the debate between atheist and non-atheist: abduction. Abduction is also

In the imagination of this child, photographed in Ames, Iowa, in 1955, these toy soldiers are as real as any flesh-and-blood humans—so real that they seem capable of marching around the room on their own. The fantasy scenario is possible because human imagination, fortunately or unfortunately, does not follow the process of inductive reasoning, which postulates general principles based on the evidence of particular instances.

known by its more descriptive name, "argument to the best explanation." Although abductive arguments draw on the inductive principle that the unobserved past, present, and future resemble the observed past and present, they are structured differently. In essence, an abductive argument examines a phenomenon or set of phenomena that has more than one possible explanation and attempts to determine which of these explanations is the best. There is no magic formula for determining which explanation is the best, but in general better explanations are simpler, more coherent, and more comprehensive than the alternatives. They are also likely to be testable in some way or have some predictive power.

Abductive reasoning, in contrast to inductive reasoning, is a method of inference that involves choosing the most likely explanation—ideally, one that is testable—for a given phenomenon. The term was originated by the mathematician, physicist, and philosopher Charles Sanders Peirce (1839–1914), who appears in this undated portrait.

Such arguments cannot be conclusive: it always remains possible that the least likely explanation turns out to be the true one. But like induction, abduction is something we cannot do without. If it fails to guarantee us a true conclusion, that is a fact we just have to live with.

When it comes to the nature of the universe and the existence of the supernatural, I think it is clear that we have to rely on abductive arguments. The reason for this is simple: there are many explanations for the way the world appears to be, and since these explanations are in conflict with each other not all of them can be true. It is wishful thinking to suppose that one or another could be proven to be the true one. To borrow a phrase from Derrida, "If things were simple word would have got around." So we can do no better than survey the options and decide which explanation fits the facts better.

It would be beyond the scope of this very short introduction to run through the merits of all the various explanations for why our world appears to us as it does. All I can do here is give a taste of why the atheist world view fits the bill as the best explanation.

First, it is simple in that it requires us to posit only the existence of the natural world. Alternatives also require us to posit the existence of an unobserved supernatural world. That extra dimension is not only metaphysically extravagant, it also makes the claims for the supernatural less testable than those for naturalism, since the supernatural world is by definition unobservable. It is true that there are those who would consider themselves religious and naturalistic, but I'm not sure to what extent such people really disagree with atheists.

The naturalistic world view of the atheist is also more coherent, because it has everything in the universe fitting into one scheme of being. Those who posit a supernatural realm have to explain how this realm and the natural one interact and coexist. Such a view is by its nature more fragmented than the unified one of the atheist.

Atheism also has great explanatory power when it comes to the existence of divergent religious beliefs. The best explanation for the fact that different religious people believe different things about God and the universe throughout the world is that religion is a human construct that does not correspond to any metaphysical reality. The alternative is that many religions exist but only one (or a few) are true. It's no good saying that all religions are different paths to the same truth: the fact has to be accepted that religions flatly contradict one other, and if one were to focus simply on what all religions agree upon one would be left with very little indeed. Hindus and Christians are not worshipping the same God, not least because Hindus do not believe in one God. Christians and Muslims fundamentally disagree in that the former see Christ as the messiah and the latter do not. Given the centrality of Christ to the Christian faith, it requires a lot of fudging of doctrine to insist that Islam and Christianity are both really true.

One can take this comparison of best explanation down to specific issues. What best explains the existence of evil in the world? You can choose between the atheist hypothesis that, as evolved creatures, there should be no expectation that the world should be a good place; or the religious explanation, which requires rather a lot of sophistical reasoning to reconcile the belief that the universe was created by a loving God with the terrible suffering and injustice found within his creation.

What best explains the correlation between consciousness and brain activity? You can choose between the atheist hypothesis that consciousness is a product of brain activity or an implausible tale about how nonmaterial thinking souls exist alongside brains and somehow interact with them, and that, further, the dependency of consciousness on brain activity miraculously disappears at death, when the soul lives on without the body.

What best explains the strength of the sex drive? You can choose between the hypothesis that it evolved because it improved the survival chances of the gene or organism and the hypothesis that God made us randy in a perverse attempt to make us more likely to sin.

Time and time again, I suggest, the better explanation for the way the world is and appears to be is that it is a natural phenomenon, and even though such explanations may not be complete, explanations that bring in a supernatural element are much less plausible and at times simply preposterous. Given that arguments to best explanation are, I have asserted, the most appropriate forms of argument concerning the fundamental nature of the world we live in, this strengthens the case for atheism.

Is Atheism a Faith Position?

We are now in a position to reject the claim often made that atheism is just a faith position like religious belief. This is an interesting claim, because if it is a faith position "just like" religious belief, then the religious are in no position to criticize atheists for their beliefs. Indeed, the religious should question the wisdom of this line of attack: if their own and competing beliefs are all just faith positions, then aren't we left with a kind of relativism, where there are no grounds for establishing the truth or falsity of any belief system and it is rather a case of believing "what works for you"?

This is particularly odd since one of the gospel verses most repeated by Christians is "I am the way, the truth, and the life. No one comes to the father except through me" (John 14:6). Jesus is not reported to have said, "I am *one* way, *one* truth, and *one* life. People can come to the father whatever way they want." Nor did he reportedly finish his speech by saying, "But that's just what I believe—your faith may be different."

We can brush these issues aside, however, for the fact is that atheism just isn't a faith position. To see why, we need to ask just what makes something a matter of faith rather than reason.

When people say that atheism is a faith position, what they tend to think is that, since there is no proof for atheism, something extra—

faith—is required to justify belief in it. But this is simply to misunderstand the role of proof in the justification for belief. It just isn't the case that we always need faith to bridge the gap between proof and belief.

The crux of the issue is the very fact I have stressed throughout my argument, that absolute proofs are not available for the vast majority of our beliefs, but that a lack of such proof is no grounds for the suspension of belief. This is because where we have a lack of absolute proof we can still have overwhelming evidence or one explanation which is far superior to the alternatives. When such grounds for belief are available we have no need for faith. It is not faith that justifies my belief that drinking fresh, clean water is good for me, but evidence. It is not faith that tells me it is not a good idea to jump out of the windows of tall buildings, but experience.

If we do want to say that faith is involved in examples such as these, since committing to any belief or action that is not strictly proven to be right requires faith, then we are really robbing the idea of faith of its distinctive character. If that is what faith is, then there is nothing to distinguish matters of faith from other beliefs. Everything becomes a matter of faith, except for perhaps belief in a few self-evident truths such as $1 + 1 = 2$.

Some may welcome that. But apart from robbing faith of any special nature, this approach also introduces a new problem. It must allow for degrees of faith, since clearly it takes less faith to believe in the refreshing power of water than it does the healing power of Christ. But then to turn around to atheists and say that their beliefs too are "just a matter of faith" becomes an empty objection. If everything is a matter of faith, this is a trivial fact. To make it nontrivial we need to be shown how the beliefs of atheists require *at least as much* faith as those of religious believers. And this is something that cannot be shown. This is because the atheist position is based on evidence and arguments to best explanation. The atheist believes in what she has good reason to believe in and doesn't believe in supernatural entities that there are few reasons to believe in, none of them strong. If this is a faith position then the amount of faith required is extremely small.

Contrast this with believers in the supernatural and we can see what a true faith position is. Belief in the supernatural is belief in what there is a lack of strong evidence to believe in. Indeed, sometimes it is belief in something that is contrary to the available evidence. Belief in life after death, for example, is contrary to the wealth of evidence we have that people are mortal animals.

This shows where I believe the real fault line between faith positions and ordinary beliefs lies. It is not about proof, but about beliefs that are in accord with evidence, experience, or logic and those that lack or are contrary to evidence, experience, or logic. Atheism is not a faith position because it is belief in nothing beyond which there is evidence and argument for; religious belief is a faith position because it goes beyond what there is evidence or argument for. That is why faith requires something "special" that ordinary belief does not.

This interpretation of faith accords with the message of the two great Christian parables of faith, the stories of Abraham and doubting Thomas. Thomas was one of Jesus's disciples and he famously refused to believe that Jesus had risen from the dead, as some of Jesus's other followers had claimed. Note that he did not have faith that Jesus had died. Rather he lacked faith that he had risen from the dead. The asymmetry is due to the fact that it requires no faith to believe that to which all the evidence points, but it does require faith to believe in something which flies in the

The apostle Thomas needed physical proof of Jesus's identity to believe that his Lord had been resurrected from the dead. The biblical scene in which Thomas examines Jesus's hands is depicted in this sixteenth-century Venetian painting.

face of experience and evidence. Thomas only believes when he is shown Jesus and told to place his hands in his wounds. The moral of the story is that "blessed are those who have not seen and yet have believed" (John 20:29). Thus Christianity endorsed the principle that it is good to believe what you have no evidence to believe, a rather convenient maxim for a belief system for which there is no good evidence.

Abraham was asked to sacrifice his only son to God, in order to test his faith. In Kierkegaard's penetrating analysis of this story, the reason why this is such a great test of faith is not because of the killing as such. After all, if God wants it, it must be good, and if you truly believe you know that you and your son will be safe in the long run. Rather, it is a test of faith because it flies in the face of everything Abraham knows about God, morality, and goodness. Reason and experience all point to the fact that God would never command such a human sacrifice. And yet it seems he has done so. Is Abraham deluded? Is God trying to test him a different way—is he supposed to defy the order and so prove his goodness? Or is it not God asking him at all, but the devil? Abraham requires faith to go ahead because what he is asked to do defies reason.

The status of atheist and religious belief are thus quite different. Only religious belief requires faith because only religious belief postulates the existence of entities which we have no good evidence to believe exist. It is a simple error to suppose that just because atheist beliefs are also "unproven" or "uncertain" that they too require faith. Faith does not plug the gap between reasons to believe and certain proof. Rather it is what supports beliefs that lack the ordinary support of evidence or argument.

The awful moment (described in Genesis) just before Abraham sacrifices Isaac is depicted in this woodcut from the Nuremberg Chronicle, an illustrated world history published in 1493. Kierkegaard's interpretation of the story emphasizes the extent to which Abraham's faith counters all reason.

And that is why, as the traditional religious texts tell us, faith is not as easy as ordinary belief. Or, as atheists tell us, why faith is foolish.

Place Your Bets

One of the most curious arguments for religious belief is Pascal's wager. The wager starts with the supposition that we cannot be sure that God exists or does not exist. It concludes that in such a position of uncertainty, it is better to believe than not believe, since the risks of nonbelief (eternal damnation) are greater than the risks of belief (wasting some of our time being devout); and the rewards of belief if God exists (eternal life) are greater than the rewards of nonbelief (more fun on this Earth) if he does not.

Blaise Pascal (1623–62) believed that a person has less to lose by believing in God than by not believing. However, for many atheists, the strength of reason overrides the doubt that Pascal felt. This statue of Pascal resides in the Louvre's Cour Napoleon, or central courtyard.

The wager is rigged because no probabilities are attached to the various outcomes. Most atheists would judge that the chances that there is a God who would condemn us to hell if we refuse to worship him are so small that it is not worth taking the bet of believing in him. But perhaps a greater problem is that, with so many religions in the world, the bet still doesn't tell us which religion to follow. Indeed, might not God be more angry with those who worship in the wrong way than with those who don't worship at all?

So let's replay Pascal's wager and see what a betting person should really do. The initial question is this: let us admit the possibility that a good, all-knowing, all-loving God exists. Given this possibility, what is it that we should do? Surely the first priority for such a being must be goodness. If there is any afterlife selection, then surely the main criterion must be virtue. So the best bet would be to act well. It does seem unlikely that such a God would send people to hell: after all, we know that most people who do terrible things are damaged individuals, often with terrible childhoods. Sending them to hell would seem rather cruel—a loving God would surely reform them. And reform is not best achieved by torture, as penal reformers constantly point out. So our fear of hell should be pretty small.

What about worship? It does seem pretty odd to suggest that the supreme being demands that we little people worship him. After all, God isn't insecure, is he? And with all the different religions available, it is hard to see how we could make an informed choice about the best way to worship anyway.

What about belief in him? If God exists, then he gave us our intelligence. If we use this intelligence to conclude that he doesn't exist, it would be a bit rich of him to turn around and chastise us. We could rightly plead, "God, I used the gifts you gave to me to try and decide what was best. I concluded you didn't exist. Surely you're not going to penalize me for doing my best with the meager intellectual instrument you gave me?"

So, if God does exist, the most likely scenario is that he cares most about our goodness, would help reform us if we were bad, and would be big enough to not really care if we don't worship him or believe in him. So if we want to make a bet as insurance against the possibility of God's existence, then we should be good, and the rest doesn't really matter. Atheist, agnostic, or believer, it is hard to see why an omnipotent deity would favor some over the others, and we risk making a big mistake if we opt for one specific kind of religious doctrine over another. The conclusion of the wager should thus be no more than E.T.'s law: "be good." Atheists are well poised to follow it, as we shall see in the next chapter.

Conclusion

In order to see the force of the argument for atheism it is necessary to think very carefully about the nature of arguments from experience and to the best explanation, and the difference between faith positions and ordinary beliefs. Once those issues have been cleared up, however, the case can be summarized simply. Atheism is the position which is best supported by the evidence and the one which offers the best overall explanation for why the world is as it is and appears to be. In contrast to faith positions, it does not require us to believe in anything which goes beyond reason or evidence, or indeed in anything which is contrary to them. The fact that we cannot be one hundred percent certain that atheism is true is only grounds for not being dogmatic in our beliefs. It is not a ground for agnosticism, nor for believing that atheism is a faith position just like religious belief.

I suspect that two major questions will still be nagging believers at this stage. For all my talk of best explanations and evidence, people may still think that atheism leaves two major issues totally unexplained. One is morality. If atheism is true, then what of right and wrong? The second concerns meaning or purpose. Atheism may explain a lot, but surely it cannot explain what the meaning and purpose of life is. And if this is unexplained, atheism cannot be the best explanation of the human situation. I will address both these concerns in the next two chapters. But for now, I should point out that, even if atheism did mean the end of ethics and that there is no purpose to human life, that is not an argument against atheism. It may just be that the most honest and truthful account of the world we live in reveals that morality and meaning in life are no more than wishful thinking. Fortunately, as I will go on to show, that is not the case. But in order to think about these issues clearly, we at least have to acknowledge the possibility that there is a mismatch between what we want to be true and what is true.

THREE

Atheist Ethics

·

Laws and Lawgivers

DOSTOEVSKY'S IVAN KARAMAZOV may have said, "Without God, anything is permitted," but I bet he never tried parking in central London on a Saturday afternoon.

This chapter is all about the truths that lie behind this joke, concerning the authority of moral law and the idea that divine authority is required to uphold it. I will argue that Ivan Karamazov was either wrong or not talking about ethics. Morality is more than possible without God, it is entirely independent of him. That means atheists are not only more than capable of leading moral lives, they may even be able to lead more moral lives than religious believers who confuse

Even without God, Dostoevsky's character Ivan Karamazov, an atheist and rationalist whose ethics didn't depend on a moralizing deity, would have found many things difficult—not to mention impermissible—were he to be dropped into this scene in London's Haymarket.

divine law and punishment with right and wrong. These conclusions run counter to much received wisdom, but the arguments that lead to them are reasonably clear and straightforward.

To begin with we need to consider why so many people think God is necessary for morality. One way in which this supposed necessity is expressed is that in order for there to be moral law there has to be some kind of lawgiver, and, ultimately, a judge. An analogy can be made with human law, which requires a legislature to make law—usually a parliament—and a judiciary to uphold it. Without these two institutions—both embodied in the moral case in God—law is impossible.

The problem with this argument is that it confuses two separate things—law and morality. Law certainly does require a legislature and judiciary. But the existence of both does not guarantee that the laws enacted and enforced will be just and good laws. One can have immoral laws as well as moral ones. What is required for just laws is for the legislature and judiciary to act within the confines of morality. Morality is thus separate from law. It is the basis upon which just laws are enacted and enforced; it is not constituted by the laws themselves.

Where then does this morality come from? It is tempting to say that moral law has its own lawgiver and judiciary. But the same questions that were asked about the law can be asked about the moral law: what is it that guarantees moral laws are indeed moral? It must be because the moral-law enactors and enforcers are acting within the confines of morality. But this then makes morality prior to any moral legislature or judiciary. To put it another way, the only thing that can show that a lawgiver is moral is that his or her laws conform to a moral standard which is independent of the moral lawgiver. So if the lawgiver is God, God's laws will only be moral if they conform to moral principles which are independent of God.

In the Judeo-Christian tradition, the figure of Moses—who, according to the Bible, received the Ten Commandments directly from God—is traditionally known as the "great lawgiver" and is often pictured holding two stone tablets containing God's edicts for correct behavior. To an atheist, however, principles of morality remain independent of any divine entity.

Plato made this point extremely clearly in a dialogue called *Euthyphro*, after which the following dilemma was named. Plato's protagonist Socrates posed the question, do the gods choose what is good because it is good, or is the good good because the gods choose it? If the first option is true, that shows that the good is independent of the gods (or in a monotheistic faith, God). Good just is good and that is precisely why a good God will always choose it. But if the second option is true, then that makes the very idea of what is good arbitrary. If it is God's choosing something alone that makes it good, then what is there to stop God choosing torture, for instance, and thus making it good? This is of course absurd, but the reason why it is absurd is that we believe that torture is wrong and *that is why* God would never choose it. To recognize this, however, is to recognize that we do not need God to determine right and wrong. Torture is not wrong *just because* God does not choose it.

To my mind, the Euthyphro dilemma is a very powerful argument against the idea that God is required for morality. Indeed, it goes further and shows that God cannot be the source of morality without morality becoming something arbitrary. There are attempts to wiggle off the prongs of the dilemma's forks, but like a trapped air bubble, pushing the problem down at one point only makes it resurface at another. For instance, some think the way out of the dilemma is to say that God just is good, so the question the dilemma poses is ill-formed. If God and good are the same thing then we cannot ask whether God chooses good because it is good—the very question separates what must come together.

This bust of Plato is a Roman copy of a Greek original from the fourth century. It resides in the Vatican Museum—an ironic location, as many atheists see Plato's dialogue *Euthyphro* as constituting an excellent argument for God's independence from any notions of morality.

But the Euthyphro dilemma can be restated in another way to challenge this reply. We can ask, is God good because to be good just is to be whatever God is; or is God good because God has all the properties of goodness? If we choose the former answer we again find that goodness is arbitrary, since it would be whatever God happened to be, even if God were a sadist. So we must choose the second option: God is good because he has all the properties of goodness. But this means the properties of goodness can be specified independently of God and so the idea of goodness does not in any way depend upon the existence of God. Hence there is no reason why a denial of God's existence would necessarily entail a denial of the existence of goodness.

Right and wrong, goodness and badness, thus do not depend on the existence of God. Indeed, in order for the idea that God is good to carry any moral force, ideas of goodness need to be independent of God. Otherwise, the distinction between right and wrong becomes arbitrary.

How then do we account for the widespread belief that "without God, anything is permitted"? I think we can trace this back to a misplaced view of morality which follows the legalistic model I outlined earlier. Our religious heritage has left us with a view of morality as a set of rules which we follow in order to be rewarded (eventually)

The threat of going to hell as punishment for disobedient behavior is still a powerful incentive for many religious people to act in a moral and ethical way. This illumination from *Les Très Riches Heures du Duc de Berry*, a fifteenth-century book of hours, or devotional book, shows Lucifer torturing the unfortunate souls in his domain.

and do not transgress in order to avoid punishment. No matter what is taught in Sunday schools about virtue's own rewards, the threats of punishment, more than promises of rewards even, have been most psychologically effective in getting people to rein in their baser instincts. To believe that God is always watching you and will punish you for any wrongdoing is a very good way of avoiding doing anything contrary to the Church's teachings.

Take away these threats, however, and what is to stop you doing something wrong? Without God, anything is permitted only in the sense that there is no divine authority who will make sure you are punished for any wrongdoing. But that is neither the end of morality nor the end of civilized behavior. The joke about parking at the start of this chapter illustrates the point that human beings are just as able to make and enforce prohibitions as gods. Everything will be permitted only if we abandon ourselves to anarchy, and there is no reason why people would want to do that just because they do not believe in God.

More profoundly, it is an odd morality that thinks that one can only behave ethically if one does so out of fear of punishment or promise of reward. The person who doesn't steal only out of fear of being caught is not a moral person, merely a prudent one. The truly moral person is the one who has the opportunity to steal without being caught but still does not do so.

I have argued that morality and religious belief are separate. If I am right, then the average ethical atheist actually appears to have more moral merit than the average ethical religious believer. The reason for this is that religion, with its threat of punishment and promise of reward, introduces a nonmoral incentive to be moral that is absent in atheism.

One perceived problem with a godless morality is the degree of personal choice it seems to leave the individual. If there is no single moral authority, then do we all become sovereigns of our own privatized moralities? Many find this worrying, but in fact individual choice is an inescapable part of morality whether one believes in God or not.

Morality and Choice

I have already mentioned Kierkegaard's *Fear and Trembling* as a study of faith, but it is also a deep study in the inescapability of personal choice. It is this aspect of the work that is most responsible for Kierkegaard's reputation as the "father of existentialism." Existentialist thinkers are a pretty disparate bunch, comprising Christians, atheists, communists, fascists, free spirits. and pretty much everything in between. What unites them is a belief in the inescapability and centrality of individual choice and freedom in human life. Their message is that you are always making choices, even when you try and pretend that you have not chosen, and that these choices carry with them responsibility. For instance, I might try and avoid making a choice by asking someone else to choose for me. But this does not mean I haven't chosen, it just means my choice has moved from being directly about my

Søren Kierkegaard (1813–55) was a fierce critic of the established Christian church in Denmark and an influential thinker whose work was a precursor of what has come to be known as Existentialism. This early-nineteenth-century portrait was painted by the artist Luplau Janssen.

final action to being about the means of making the selection. I cannot avoid my responsibility for what I go on to do: having chosen to follow the advice of someone else, I am as responsible for so doing as if I had chosen without that advice. After all, I could always choose to accept or reject the choice made for me.

Kierkegaard's retelling of the story of Abraham illustrates this point. Abraham is commanded by God to sacrifice his only son, Isaac. On the divine command model of morality—that moral law comes directly from God—it seems that Abraham has no choice: he has to obey. But it would not be a great display of Abraham's faith and goodness if he just went ahead and killed his son without any thought at all. There are at least two choices he needs to make. The first is a kind of epistemological choice: he has to decide whether the command he has received is authentic. How can people know that what they seem to have been told by God is really an instruction from God and not one from an inner voice or an evil demon? The problem is that no evidence or logic can settle this question conclusively. At the end of the day Abraham has to decide whether he personally is convinced or not. That is his choice.

The second choice is a moral one: does he follow the command? In a wonderful Woody Allen short story, Abraham thinks the answer to this is obvious: "To question the Lord's word is one of the worst things a person can do." However, when he goes ahead and takes his son to sacrifice, God is outraged that Abraham took his joke suggestion seriously. Abraham protests that at least his willingness to sacrifice his son shows he loves God. God replies that all it really proves is "that some men will follow any order no matter how asinine as long as it comes from a resonant, well-modulated voice."

The actor, director, and writer Woody Allen, more than one hundred years after Kierkegaard, also interpreted the biblical story of Abraham and Isaac in terms of individual moral choice. An avowed atheist, Allen is the source of many memorable bon mots on the subject of God and religion. In the autobiographical 1980 film *Stardust Memories*, when his character is called an atheist, Allen responds: "To you, I'm an atheist. To God, I'm the loyal opposition." Allen is pictured here in 2005.

The Allen story is a comic retelling of Kierkegaard's philosophical retelling of the Bible story, and both make many of the same points. The most striking idea is that Abraham cannot evade his moral responsibility by simply following orders. We should be alert to this since the terrible human propensity to do awful things just as long as they are commanded by someone in authority was particularly evident in the twentieth century. Abraham's choice to obey the order is not just a choice to accept or reject God's authority. It is a moral choice to decide whether what he is being asked to do is right or wrong. After all, surely it would not be right to do what God commanded (assuming you were satisfied that God really had commanded it) no matter what it was. If God asked you to lower an innocent person into acid inch by inch, killing them slowly in terrible pain, would that be okay? Of course it wouldn't. Religious believers are sure that God would never ask such a thing (although the Old Testament God does ask for some pretty bloodthirsty deeds to be carried out). But the point is not that God might ask people to do such a thing, it is that the hypothetical example shows that following or rejecting a command given to you by another, even God, is a matter of personal choice which carries moral responsibility.

The atheist and the believer are therefore in the same boat. Neither can avoid choosing which moral values to follow and taking responsibility for them. The atheist has the advantage, however, of being much more aware of this fact. It is easy for the religious believer to think that they can avoid choice just by listening to the advice of their holy men (it is usually men) and sacred texts. But since adopting this attitude can lead to suicide bombing, bigotry, and other moral wrongs, it should be obvious that it does not absolve one of moral responsibility. So although the idea of individuals making moral choices for themselves may sound unpalatable to those used to thinking about morality deriving from a single authority, none of us can avoid making such choices.

The famed English social satirist and cartoonist William Hogarth (1697–1764) created many works in which he pointed out the religious hypocrisy of his day. This one, entitled *Credulity, Superstition, and Fanaticism*, aims a pointed barb at Methodism. As Hogarth so creatively points out, belonging to a religion does not mean that a person can avoid moral wrongs.

Sources of Morality

So far I have argued that religion and morality are separate, and that even if you still think God is the main source of moral guidance, that does not mean you can avoid making choices about which moral principles to adopt for yourself. We need to go further, however, if we are to make a persuasive case that atheist morality is possible. It is not enough to show that religion cannot be the source of morality: we need to show what can be. It is not enough to show that we have to make moral choices for ourselves: we need to show that such choices carry moral weight.

When it comes to saying what the source of morality is, however, there are no easy answers. The difficulty can be seen by considering the strangeness of the question, "Why should I be moral?" This question can have two kinds of answer. One could provide a nonmoral answer. For instance, one might say you ought to be moral because you will happier if you are or God will punish you if you are not. These are what we can call prudential reasons to be moral. The trouble is that sincerely believing in these reasons appears to undermine morality rather than support it. Acting morally because it is one's own best interest to do so does not seem to be acting morally at all. Morality is about acting in the best interests of others and oneself.

However, if we give a moral answer to the question, such as "be moral because that's what you ought to do," we encounter the problem of circularity in our justification. Since the question is about why we ought to be moral at all, we cannot help ourselves to a moral reason as part of the answer, since that would beg the question. We can only offer a moral reason for action if we are already persuaded of the merits of morality.

So we face a dilemma. If we want to know why we should be moral, our answer will either beg the question (if it offers a moral reason) or will

In this photograph, taken on
September 15, 2001, a New York
City fireman calls for ten more
rescue workers to make their way
into the rubble of the World Trade
Center—an action that signifies the
generosity, empathy, and altruism
demonstrated by so many of the
people who risked their own lives to
save others in the aftermath of the
terrorist attack.

undermine the morality of morality (if it offers a nonmoral one). This is not just a problem for atheists. The same logic holds for everyone. The reasons to obey a God-given morality will either themselves be moral or nonmoral, and thus the same problem is faced by the religious believer.

The existence of this problem is not an argument against morality, however. It is merely a caution against the expectation that one can hope to find a simple source for morality, a reason to be moral that every rational person should recognize. I would argue that such a source cannot be found. The best attempt to find such a source is the Kantian endeavor to show that acting morally is required by rationality, which we will look at shortly. But despite their inventiveness and ingenuity, such attempts do not, I think, ultimately succeed.

What then can we put in place of such a source? I believe that at the very root of morality is a kind of empathy or concern for the welfare of others, a recognition that their welfare also counts. This is, for most of us, a basic human instinct. Total indifference to the welfare of others is not normal human behavior, it is symptomatic of what we would normally call mental illness. Its most extreme form is that of the psychopath, who has no sense of the inner life of others at all. This recognition of the value of others is not a logical premise but a psychological one. If we accept it, then we have the starting point for all the thinking and reasoning about ethics that help us to make better decisions and become better people. But the truth of the premise, the fundamental conviction that others do count, is not something that can be demonstrated by logic. This is part of what Hume was getting at when he said "reason is, and ought only to be, the slave of the passions." Moral reasoning can only get going if we have a basic altruistic impulse to begin with.

I should briefly mention an alternative view, which is that we should just accept that the reasons to be moral are themselves nonmoral. Morality, on this view, is a kind of enlightened self-interest. Recognizing this does undermine the romantic view that morality is about a lack of self-interest, but some argue it need not completely undermine morality. Giving money to charity, for example, is no less moral because it is done out of enlightened self-interest. What matters is that we act well. It need not matter that the ultimate justifications for so doing are selfish.

I am not persuaded by this because it does seem to me to be an indispensable part of ethics that self-interest is not sovereign. At best, the view of morality as enlightened self-interest gives us reasons not to engage in antisocial behavior or to do things that benefit us in the short run but have greater long-term costs. But that is not morality. Morality always contains the possibility of requiring one to act against one's own interests. If I am never prepared to sacrifice some self-interest, then I do not think I can ever be truly moral.

We can now return to the problems posed at the start of this section. If God isn't the source of morality, what is? I would suggest it is a basic concern for the welfare of others, a concern that is not based on rational argument but empathy and, for want of a better phrase, our shared humanity. The second problem was, if it is up to us to make our own moral choices, do these choices carry any moral weight? I would argue that they do, because if we recognize the need to think about the moral dimension to our actions, then morality has to matter. The fact that we are left with choices to make cannot make it matter any less. The seriousness of morality derives from the seriousness with which we take the need to account for the interests of others and ourselves. It does not derive from the system we use to help us take these interests into account. Morality's seriousness is not diminished if moral decisions are freely chosen by us rather than dictated to us by laws laid down in heaven.

Moral Thinking

The overall framework of my discussion in this chapter has been the existentialist insight that we cannot avoid responsibility for the choices we make and that therefore we have to in some sense "create" values for ourselves. The discussion has largely been about metaethics—the general nature, basis, and structure of morality. If we are to move on from here, however, and think about the specific content of morality—what we should actually do—we need to do some further thinking. What I am going to do next is simply sketch three broad approaches to moral reasoning that have been dominant in the history of Western philosophy. All of these demonstrate how rich secular discussions of ethics can be. They show how the resources of good moral reasoning are equally available to the atheist and the religious believer.

Rather than view these as rival theories, I suggest we should see them all as resources we can draw upon to help in our moral reasoning. Of course, a "pick and mix" approach has

The Aristotelian theory of ethics is one of three secular approaches that scholars identify as being central to any discussion of the subject. This bust of Aristotle is a Roman copy after a Greek bronze original by Lysippos that dates from 330 BCE.

severe limitations. Most notably, adopting one way of thinking about a moral problem might lead to a conclusion that is diametrically opposed to the conclusion reached by using another method. Nevertheless, all these approaches offer ways into moral thinking that can at least help us to think a little more about what is at stake. What we should not do is think that they are like little moral calculi that can be called into action to generate an appropriate response to any moral dilemma.

Most introductory ethics classes in philosophy would distinguish between Aristotelian, Kantian, and Utilitarian ethics. However, since it is my claim that we can draw on all three and that we should not see them as hermetically sealed rival theories, I am going to focus on the distinctive features of each rather than consider them as complete theories. This will make it much easier to see how it is possible to draw on all three without loss of intellectual integrity. These three characteristics are the emphases on human flourishing, consequences, and the universal form of moral law.

Human Flourishing

If you flick through Aristotle's great work of moral philosophy, the *Nichomachean Ethics*, you might notice something that looks strange to modern eyes. At one point, Aristotle asks what the right

Aristotle's *Nicomachean Ethics* sets forth the philosopher's principles in a series of ten books based on notes from his lectures at the ancient Greek Lyceum, just outside Athens. These lectures were either edited by or dedicated to Aristotle's son, Nicomachus. Pictured here is the title page of a bilingual edition of the *Nicomachean Ethics* printed in 1566.

number of friends to have is and whether or not it is possible to be friends with bad people. But how can the number of friends we have be a concern of ethics?

Understand this and you have understood what is very different about the Ancient Greek conception of ethics compared to some popular modern conceptions of morality. We tend to think of morality in terms of prohibitions and obligations. There are things we ought to do and things we ought not to do, and living a moral life consists in following these rules. Our broader life goals, such as success, happiness, or finding the perfect pizza, are then pursued within these constraints.

This modern conception separates out the idea of a life going well for a given individual and that person following moral rules. This distinction did not exist in Aristotle's ethics, nor in many of the ethics of other Ancient Greek thinkers. For them, ethics just was about what is required for a human life to go well or to "flourish." What we would now recognize as moral rules were based on the idea that following such maxims was required if one's life was to go well.

Because ethics was approached in this way, the list of recommendations Aristotle made included some things we would think were obviously about ethics and some things which we would not. So the good person—one whose life is going well—will be prudent, have a close circle of not too many friends, show courage, be just, spend money wisely, and be amiable and witty.

A central insight of Aristotle's was that in order to live such a life one has to cultivate certain dispositions of character. He recognized that we are creatures of habit and that the best way of ensuring we act well is for us to practice doing good things, so that we then do them without having to think about it. So moral education is about instilling

One of the qualities that Aristotle urges his listeners to embrace is prudence, a non-religious attribute that later became one of the cardinal virtues of Christian theology. This photograph shows part of an allegorical statue of Prudence in the Basilica of Sant'Eustorgio in Milan, Italy. The sculptor endowed her with three faces, symbolizing her consideration of the past, present, and future. Two of the three faces appear here.

virtuous habits, while moral theorizing can be undertaken only once we are mature and developed.

One important question is whether Aristotle's ethics ignores the distinction between morality and self-interest or shows that the division is illusory. It would be nice to think that just as long as we do what is genuinely required for our lives to flourish then we will always do the right thing by others. But this may be too optimistic a view. After all, it has to be remembered that Aristotle was writing for a male, slave-owning class who did not take into account the interests of those lower down the social ladder. There is no hand-wringing in Aristotle about the slave's ability to lead a flourishing life: slaves are just ignored. So there are at least grounds for concern that Aristotle's approach only meets the interest of some and not all, and that therefore it fails to provide a true morality.

Nevertheless, it is heartening to see just how far one can go with Aristotle's approach. Just by thinking about what is required for a life to go well, we end up with a picture of a virtuous life which is in almost all respects an extremely moral one. Greed, anger, maliciousness, petty self-interest, and so forth do not enter into the life of Aristotle's flourishing person. For your life to go well for you, you cannot afford to be in the grip of these destructive forces.

So here is a first step in moral thinking. Forget any transcendental lawgiver or divine source of morality. Just think about what is needed for a human life to go well and you will soon find that most of what we recognize as morality comes into play.

A morality play is a type of allegorical theatrical entertainment that aims to demonstrate the benefits of acting in a moral way. Typically, the protagonist of the story encounters personifications of various moral attributes who prompt him to choose a life of good over a life of evil. In the Middle Ages, the plays were highly religious in nature, but by the fifteenth and sixteenth centuries they represented a shift toward a secular European theater. One such play is *Mundus et Infans* (The World and the Child). This photograph shows the title page of an edition of that play published in 1522 by the British printer Wynkyn de Worde.

If that were all we could say about morality, however, we might be a little concerned. After all, it does seem that the wicked can flourish too. Many have tried to argue that this is not so, and that, despite appearances, no one who is wicked is truly happy or content. I personally wish this were true but find it hard to believe. Life would be very easy if self-interest and living well always coincided. But I don't think they do, and that is why we need to draw upon other ways of thinking about ethics if we are to construct a credible morality.

Consequences

It is an obvious fact about actions that they have consequences. What is more, these consequences can be good or bad: they can make things better or worse. Arguably, the mere fact that we recognize this to be true is enough to get some form of morality going.

To give a simple example, if I kick someone for no reason then that causes the person pain. That pain is a bad thing which cannot in any way be outweighed by any better, good thing, because there is no reason for the kicking. Recognizing that the causing of this pain is a bad thing thus gives me a reason not to kick anyone.

It should be obvious that if we start thinking in this way we have the basis for a kind of morality, one that is usually termed consequentialist. We have reasons for not doing things that have bad consequences and we have reasons to do things that have good consequences, just because we recognize that it is better that good things happen than bad ones.

As soon as we try and build on this banal-sounding truism to construct a complete moral theory we head into difficulties. But it does not seem to me that these subsequent difficulties in any way cast doubt upon the simple observations that set us off in this direction.

For instance, consider one difficulty, which concerns the status of these reasons for action.

If we start to think about why a thing having bad consequences is a reason for not doing it we can soon see a puzzle. What kinds of reasons are they? Are they reasons that express simple facts? Is "pain is a bad thing" a kind of factual truth on a par with "lead is heavier than water"? Many philosophers have thought not. "Lead is heavier than water" is a

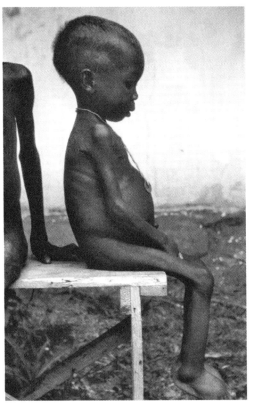

Most people, regardless of their religious affiliation or lack thereof, agree that human suffering is a bad thing, one that should be prevented if possible. But the academic and philosophical debate surrounding this issue seems inconsequential in the face of a child's pain. This girl is among many victims of kwashiorkor, a type of nutritional deficiency found in Nigerian relief camps during the Nigerian-Biafran War (1967–70).

simple, incontrovertible truth which is demonstrated by the physical sciences. In saying that it is true we are doing no more than describing the world. But when we say "pain is a bad thing" it seems we are not just describing the world, we are evaluating it. If we were simply describing the world we could say things like "pain is found to be unpleasant" or "pain is something living creatures seek to avoid," but the moment we say it is bad we move beyond the facts to making value judgments.

If this line of reasoning is correct, then any moral argument that is based on a claim that "pain is a bad thing" is not just expressing truths about the world but is making a judgment about it. And that means that moral claims are not true or false in the same way as factual claims are. Because moral claims are judgments, it is always possible for someone to disagree with them without saying something that is factually false. So if I say pain is not bad, you may disagree with me but you cannot say I have made a factual error.

There are various philosophical reasons why this question is important. But in practice I am not sure it matters one bit. All we need to get going on a broadly consequentialist way of thinking about ethics is to accept that pain is a bad thing. Now it is an interesting question whether or not "pain is a bad thing" is a fact or a judgment, but as long as we agree that pain is a bad thing, for practical purposes the question does not require an answer.

But what about people who do not accept that pain is a bad thing? Let us assume this disagreement is not on technical grounds (in other words that they refuse to assert that it is a bad thing because they believe to do so entails some philosophical commitment they do not want to sign up to). In such a circumstance I don't think we need to be concerned by the fact that our moral view does not command one hundred percent agreement. As I have already argued, morality in the end requires a personal commitment and the acceptance of responsibility. In some unusual circumstances we may be confronted with a situation where rational argument can take us no further and we are confronted with a stark disagreement: I think (unnecessary) pain is bad, you do not. In such a situation we can only stand up for our values. And since our most basic values are shared with the vast majority of other human beings, such resolution in the face of dissent is hardly fascistic.

I would not want to suggest that there aren't real problems with consequentialist thinking. Indeed, I think there are a great many and that a purely consequentialist moral system is deeply flawed. However, that does not diminish the fact that in simply accepting that bad consequences provide reasons not to do certain actions and good consequences provide reasons to do others we have one pillar upon which to build a godless morality.

Universalizability

There is something else we could say about why it is bad to cause unnecessary pain which opens the door to another powerful way of thinking about ethics. In each of our own cases we would have no problem in seeing that it is bad for us to suffer unnecessary pain. But if it is bad for us, surely it is also bad for any other creature that could suffer pain in a similar way? If that is true, we have another reason not to cause suffering to others.

This is a very natural line of thought, and versions of the principle that stands behind it have been formulated in various different ways throughout history, from Confucius's golden rule "Do not do to others what you would not want done to yourself," through Kant's categorical imperative, to parents who ask their child to consider what would happen if everyone behaved like that.

What reasons do we have to accept something like the golden rule? One reason is that we are in danger of acting inconsistently—or to put it more crudely, hypocritically—if we don't. We can see why by thinking about Kant's distinction between what he called hypothetical and categorical imperatives. An imperative is any kind of command such as "you must do X" or "you ought to do X." Some imperatives hold only with regard to some desired outcome or purpose. For example, if I'm trying to gain weight, then it might be said that I ought to have another cream cake. This "ought" carries some force only because of my desired goal of gaining weight: I *ought* to eat the cake only *if* I want to gain weight. Such an imperative is "hypothetical" in Kant's terminology, meaning that we

One of several secular approaches to the issue of ethics lies in the distinction between a hypothetical and a categorical imperative, first identified by the German philosopher Immanuel Kant (1724–1804), seen here in this undated portrait. Kant argued that moral imperatives are categorical—that is, universal—and are by definition not grounded in an individual's wish or desire.

always need to give some goal or aim to explain why we really ought to do what the imperative commands.

In contrast to these, Kant argued that moral "oughts" are categorical. I ought not to murder regardless of my aims or objectives. The prohibition is categorical, meaning that we do not need to give some goal or aim to explain why we really ought to follow it.

One of the points Kant is making is that this just is the structure of a moral rule. It is the nature of moral rules that they have the form of categorical imperatives. If this is true, then whenever we recognize that we ought to do something or ought not to do something else, we are endorsing a principle that is not relative to the particular interests, desires, or objectives of specific individuals, but universal and applicable to all. So, for example, to recognize that I ought not to be cheated is to recognize that no one ought to be cheated. To be indignant about being cheated while not worrying about cheating others is thus an example of hypocrisy: the arbitrary changing of rules to suit oneself.

We need not go as far with Kant to embrace the idea of the categorical imperative to see that some form of universalizability is both an essential feature of moral rules and a natural part of moral reasoning. All we need to get the general principle of universalizability is first to accept that certain things are good or bad if they happen to us, and second to accept that there is no rational reason why, if they are good or bad for us, then they are not also good or bad for other people in similar circumstances. If we accept these two propositions then we have some kind of rational grounding for the principle that we ought not to do unto others what we would object to them doing unto us.

As with all the moral principles I have sketched, we do not have to go too far into the details for things to get difficult and controversial. In this instance, one of the major debates is whether or not universal, categorical imperatives are somehow demanded by reason, as Kant thought, or whether or not the sense in which universalizing moral rules is rational is much weaker. For what it's worth, I think the second response is correct. But as with so many details of moral philosophy, for practical purposes these debates may not matter very much. The very basic principle of universalizability, that if we think something ought to be done in one instance then it ought to be done in other relevantly similar circumstances, commands sufficient agreement and can be used in such a wide range of moral arguments that technical problems with its formulation and justification are no obstacle to its employment in everyday moral reasoning.

Conclusion

It should now be obvious that the idea that the atheist must be an amoralist is groundless. The religious believer and the atheist share an important common ground. For both it cannot be that what is right and wrong, good or bad, is defined in terms of God or simply follows from divine command. For both, moral choices ultimately have to be made by individuals, and we cannot get others to make our moral choices for us. So whether we have religious faith or not, we have to make up our own minds about what is right and wrong.

To provide a source for morality we need to do no more than sign up to the belief that certain things have a value and that the existence of this value provides us with reasons to behave in certain ways. This very broad commitment does not entail any specific

This lithograph, appearing on the cover of the December 12, 1886, issue of *Puck* magazine, reminds readers of that year's Hospital Sunday, an appointed day on which church members throughout a given community are asked to contribute money to local hospitals. The image shows a figure representing Charity tending to a man whose arm rests in a sling with two of London's prominent hospitals in the background. Hospital Sunday notwithstanding, a person doesn't have to belong to a religious organization to donate to charitable causes.

philosophical or even religious position. It is arguably no more than the basic commitment of someone who has human feeling.

Once we have undertaken this basic commitment we have several resources to help us think about what the right thing to do is. We can think about what is required to help our own lives and the lives of others flourish. We can think about what the consequences of our actions are and avoid those that harm things we think are of value and try to do those things which benefit them. And we can recognize that to say something is good or bad in one circumstance is to say it is good or bad in any other relevantly similar circumstance, and so can strive to be consistent in our actions, or to put it another way, strive to avoid hypocrisy.

Of course, it can still be said that we can provide no logical proof that atheists ought to behave morally, but neither can we provide such a proof for theists. The mistake that is often made is to suppose that if one has religious belief, moral principles just come along with the package and there is no need to think about or justify them. Once we see through that myth, we can see why being good is a challenge for everyone, atheist or non-atheist.

Life has
meaning.

FOUR

Meaning and Purpose

●

What's the Point?

BELIEVING THE MYTH that without God everything is permitted may not in itself provide people with a reason to reject atheism, since it at least opens the gates to a certain amount of potentially desirable debauchery. What is perhaps more off-putting about atheism is the idea that without God nothing has a purpose. Sure, you can do what you want because there's no divine power there to stop you, but what is the point of doing anything at all? Why do we struggle through life—and for many people life is a struggle—if it all ends in naught? "Life's a bitch and then you die" is the nihilistic mantra of the disenchanted and disappointed who have given up belief in God and think that leaves life a vacuous tragicomedy.

The unknown epigrammatist who placed this sign on a door in Scotland must have had some reason for believing in the intrinsic significance of human life, but leaves that reason unsaid. It's hard to know whether the message is aimed at theists or atheists, but people from both camps can attest to its truth.

To answer these concerns it is necessary to go back to basics and consider the very idea of life having a meaning or purpose. The problem is that it is often assumed that there is no problem about the meaning of life for the religious. Buy into religion and meaning comes with it free. Opt out of religion, however, and you lose meaning. This line of reasoning is very similar to that which yokes together ethics and religion. It is assumed that ethics is packaged with religion and so without religion ethics becomes problematic. As we saw in the last chapter, this is simply not true and in this chapter I will argue that it is also not true that life's meaning and purpose are prepackaged together with religion. To do this I will look at how to understand the idea that life has meaning and purpose at all.

The Designer's Purpose

The French existentialist thinker Jean-Paul Sartre believed that a rejection of the idea of God left humanity with no "essence." He meant something quite specific by "essence," which he explains with the example of a paper knife. A paper knife has a clear essence, he says, because it was designed with a purpose: to cut paper. In this way, its creator endows it with an essence: the essential nature of the paper knife is to cut paper.

This idea of an essence corresponds to what some people might think of as the knife's purpose. In other words, the knife has a purpose which is its function as given to it by its creator.

Sartre argued that, since God does not exist, human beings are not like paper knives, since an intelligent designer did not create them. Thus, they lack what he called an essence. Interestingly, however, he did not conclude that human life lacked purpose or meaning, for reasons that will become clear in a little while.

For the French existentialist philosopher and writer Jean-Paul Sartre (1905–80), shown in this photograph taken on April 28, 1970, human beings lack an "essence," or specific function, in the absence of a deity. However, Sartre did not conclude from this premise that life lacks meaning.

First, however, we need to pay some attention to this idea that purpose or meaning is endowed on something by its creator. This seems to be the idea which supports the religious view that belief in God provides one automatic answer to the question of life's meaning. If we are created by God then our purpose is simply handed to us on a plate by that God, since he made us with some purpose in mind. The analogy crops up in various forms in religious discourse. For instance, people talk a little whimsically about the Bible being God's instruction manual, there to inform his creations about what they have been made for.

The problem here, however, is that on reflection this seems to provide us only with a very unsatisfactory form of meaning in life. The knife analogy shows us why. Although it is true that the knife has meaning and purpose because of its creator, this kind of purpose is hardly significant *for the knife*. Of course, the knife has no consciousness at all, and this reinforces the point that when we ascribe a purpose to something in virtue of what it was made for, this locates the significance of that purpose with the creator or the user of the object, not in the object itself.

The English novelist and essayist Aldous Huxley (1894–1963) is the author of the famed 1932 science fiction novel *Brave New World*, set in "the year of our Ford 632" (the year 2540). According to the introduction of a recent edition of the novel, Huxley's experience working at a chemical plant in England—an experience of "an ordered universe in a world of planless incoherence"—was one source of inspiration for the novel. Huxley appears here in a photograph taken in January of 1925.

Consider now a hypothetical example where the created object is conscious. Imagine a dystopian future where human beings are bred in laboratories to fulfill certain functions, rather like the scenario in Aldous Huxley's *Brave New World*. Here we can imagine a person who has been created with the purpose of cleaning lavatories. If that person were to ask what the meaning or purpose of his life were, we could say, in a sense correctly, "to clean lavatories." But to think that by doing so we had answered the important existential question about the meaning of life would be absurd. In short, a purpose or meaning given to a creature by its creator just isn't necessarily the kind of purpose or meaning that we are looking for in life when we wonder what the point of living is *for us*. If the only point in living is to serve *somebody else's* purposes, then we cease to be valuable beings in our own right and we merely become tools for others, like paper knives or cloned workers.

This is why a belief in a creator God does not automatically provide life with a meaning. It can, however, satisfy some people's desire for

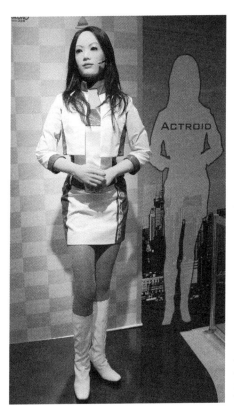

Aldous Huxley's vision of a world in which human beings are created in a laboratory to fulfill a specific purpose has perhaps come true with the introduction of the Actroid, a robot developed by the Japanese company Kokoro, Inc. The machine, designed to demonstrate products at trade shows, speaks four languages—Japanese, Chinese, Korean, and English. The droid shown here, a kind of mechanical emcee, was unveiled at the 2005 International Robot Exhibition in Tokyo, Japan.

meaning in one of two ways. The first is if people decide that they are happy just to do God's will. Serving God is a good enough purpose in life for them. This seems odd to me, since I find it hard to imagine why God would want to create creatures like us solely to serve him: it's not as though he's in need of domestic help or anything like that. It also seems unnervingly close in attitude to the people who for many centuries thought it was simply their role in life to work for the aristocracy and the upper classes. To take pride in one's lowly position and to see that as conferring meaning on one's life seems to me indicative of what Nietzsche called "slave morality": sanctifying what is in reality an unfortunate position so as to make that place seem much more desirable than it really is.

This likeness of the German philosopher Friedrich Nietzsche first appeared in the German magazine *Pan* in 1899. Nietzsche is famous for, among other things, uttering the opinion in several of his works that "God is dead," by which he meant dead not in the physical sense but dead in the sense that religion is no longer capable of serving as a source of moral authority.

This seems to be an example of what Sartre called "bad faith": pretending to oneself that things are other than they really are in order to avoid uncomfortable truths.

A second way out for the religious is to simply trust that God has a purpose for us which is genuinely a purpose *for us* rather than something we do *for him*. We may not know what that is but we've got eternity to find out, so what's the rush? This is a perfectly coherent position but as with much else in religion it has to be recognized that it requires the religious to take something on complete blind trust, or, as they prefer to put it, on faith. To adopt this position is to admit that the religious actually don't have any clue what the meaning or purpose of life is, but that they simply trust God has one for them. And there is still the troubling doubt that a meaning that is given to us by others isn't necessarily the kind of meaning which makes life meaningful for us. The religious just have to have faith that their purpose is not the equivalent of cleaning paradise's lavatories for eternity.

This thought-provoking graphic provides a concise visual summary of the artist's take on human evolution. It seems to indicate that we evolved for a very specific—and perhaps undesirable—purpose. The image was spotted on a wall on Vali-ye Asr Avenue in Tehran, Iran.

Purpose as Goal

So God or no God, if life is to be really meaningful it must be so in a way which speaks to our own projects, needs, or desires and not just the purposes of whatever or whoever created us. This is why, incidentally, the theory of evolution doesn't provide life with any meaning either. Evolution tells us that the reason why we are here is, in some sense, to replicate DNA. But this is a purely external explanation of why we exist and what biological function we fulfill. This no more explains the meaning of life than saying you were conceived so that your parents could claim extra child benefit. It gives part of the causal story of why you were born; it doesn't tell you why your life is significant, if indeed it is.

If we start thinking about life's meaning independently of the purposes of a creator, a natural way to start off is by thinking about our own

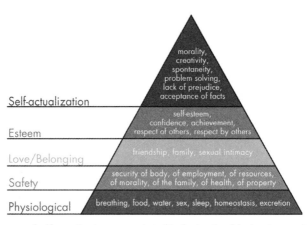

The concept of self-actualization was popularized in the theories of the American psychologist Abraham Maslow (1908–70). In Maslow's view, human needs can be organized into a pyramid, at which the most basic needs appear at the bottom. Only when a person has met the needs on the lower strata can self-actualization take place.

purposes or goals. It does seem that many people do look at life's meaning in this way. They talk about what they want to have achieved by the age of thirty, fifty, or sixty-five with the implicit assumption that reaching these goals will fulfill them and make their lives meaningful.

One interesting point to note here is that in most cases people do not have the idea that these goals or purposes were given to them by God. It is true that you sometimes hear, for example, athletes saying things like "God put me on Earth to win the 200-meter Olympic gold medal," but most of their peers will admit that winning is something they want and does God no favors at all. In general, when people set themselves life goals they choose these goals themselves, and that is actually an important part of why those goals are meaningful for them. What people are doing is trying to achieve some form of "self-actualization." They set goals which they see as developing and fulfilling their potential so that they can become in a sense more than they now are. So, for example, people with a talent for music might set goals which, if achieved, will show that they have developed their musical abilities to their fullest potential and hence that they have become more complete or developed individuals than they once were.

This idea that we can choose our own purposes and goals and thus be the authors of our own meaning is an important one and I will return to it shortly. But first we should rec-ognize some potential problems with seeing life's meaning as comprising one or more goals we set ourselves. If we are too goal-orientated two risks confront us.

The first is that we simply do not achieve our goal. In areas such as ath-letics, it is inevitable that many more people fail to achieve their goals than actually do so. But if a failure to hit the target is closely linked or is even a major part of what makes life mean-ingful for a person, then such a failure could be personally catastrophic.

The second risk is that, having achieved our goals, life then becomes meaningless. This is actually some-thing that does happen to some people who become very focused on one particular goal that takes many

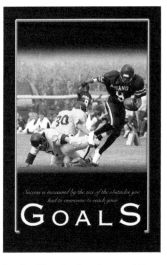

People with goal-oriented personalities find meaning in the pursuit of their life's ambition. This inspirational poster, created by the U.S. Air Force's communications squadron at Aviano Air Base in Italy, is clearly intended for goal-oriented individuals. The caption reads: "Success is measured by the size of the obstacles you had to overcome to reach your goals."

years to achieve. You will hear many a person say something like, "I spent my whole life working toward achieving this and now that I've succeeded I don't know what to do with myself." Often, since these people have very goal-directed personalities, the response is to set another goal and get back on the treadmill. This just highlights the problem of tying meaning too closely to goal achievement: life can never be truly satisfying except in those few moments around the achievement of each goal. At all other times, you are either working for the future goal or looking back on its past attainment.

The problem can be posed more philosophically by considering what makes anything worthwhile. For example, since I lead an exciting life, today I'm going to buy some groceries. Why would I spend valuable time doing something so boring? The reason is that I need food to eat. But why should I bother eating? Two reasons: one is that I like it and the other is that I need food to live. So why bother living? And so on.

In this simple series of "why" questions two types of answer can be given. One explains my actions in terms of another, more fundamental goal: to get food, to live. With this kind of answer, however, it is always possible to ask a further "why" question. Why bother eating? Why bother living? In order to put a halt to the series of why questions we have to provide a reason which is sufficient in itself and does not simply relate to some further goal or purpose. One such reason I gave is that I eat because I like it. If you were to then ask why I like it, or why I should do what I like, then you have not really understood what it means to enjoy doing something. To enjoy doing something is itself a good enough reason to do it, provided it doesn't harm others or yourself, or prevent you from doing something more important, and various other similar caveats. So if I say I enjoy eating to explain why I am tucking into a plate of aloo gobi, there is no need or sense in asking a further why question.

If we apply this principle more widely, then we can see how, if we ask why we do anything in life, eventually we have to end up with things that are valuable in themselves and are not done simply to meet some further aim or goal. If we become too goal-fixated we risk missing this vital point.

That does not mean that the achievement of goals cannot contribute to life's meaning. Goals can play a very important role in giving meaning to our lives. But they fulfill this role best if they satisfy two conditions. The first is that we find the process of achieving them itself meaningful and rewarding. That way, the time we spend working toward the goal is meaningful even if we do not finally achieve it. The second is that the achieving of the goal itself leads to something which is of enduring value to us. That way, once we have achieved our goal, we do not suddenly find our lives empty.

A further danger with thinking too much about goals and achievements is that it might make the lives of too many people seem meaningless. The fact is that many people, perhaps the majority, are not goal-directed or hungry for success. What most people want is companionship, a job they enjoy, and sufficient money for a good quality of life. Given all those things, life seems meaningful enough, since that overall package is a good in itself. Does it really make sense to ask, "Why would you want to do a job you enjoy all day and then go home to someone you love and fill your leisure time as you please?" Isn't the person who asks such a question missing something?

Life as Its Own Answer

We have been led to the view that life's ultimate purpose must be something which is good in itself and is not just something that serves as a link in a never-ending series of purposes. This is one reason why atheists can claim that life is more meaningful for them than it is for many religious people who see this world as a kind of preparation for the next. For these people, life isn't really valuable in itself at all. It is like a coin which can be exchanged for a good that really does count: the afterlife. This merely postpones the question about what makes life worth living, however, since it doesn't tell us why life in heaven is

For many religious people, the earthly world is only a way station on the road to the perfections of heaven. This roadside billboard was photographed in 2003.

meaningful in itself but life on Earth isn't. Once again, it seems religion does not so much provide an answer as ask us to accept on trust that an answer will be forthcoming.

Since at some stage life must become worth living for its own sake or else it has no meaning or value in itself at all, the atheist's desire to try and find what makes this life worth living rather than hoping that the next one will be better seems sensible and prudent, especially given the evidence that this is the only life we're going to get anyway.

But what makes life worth living? Any short answer will sound trite, but there really is no mystery about it. Ray Bradbury put it pithily in his short story "And the Moon Be Still as Bright." This tells of Martians rather than humans, but the moral of the story translates:

> The Martians realized that they asked the question "Why live at all?" at the height of some period of war or despair, when there was no answer. But once the civilization calmed, quieted, and wars ceased, the question became senseless in a new way. Life was now good and needed no argument.

When times are hard and life is going badly, life can seem pointless. But when life is good there is no need to question. As in the example above, if one's work and home life are going well, it is in a way senseless to ask why such a life is worth living. The person living it just knows it is.

Of course this really isn't good enough as an answer in itself since it doesn't tell us what to say to others or ourselves when life isn't going well. For most of us, life is pretty much a mixed bag, and periods where

The works of writer Ray Bradbury (b. 1920), who is perhaps best known for his science-fiction novel *Fahrenheit 451*, raise thought-provoking questions about the nature of human existence outside the context of a religious framework.

everything is going just fine and dandy are quite rare and brief. But what is true about Bradbury's sentiments is that the essence of the answer can only be rooted in the fact that life can be worth living in itself, even in difficult times, and there is no need for it to serve any other purpose. Furthermore, recognizing that life is its own answer to the question of why we should live is essential if we are to confront the reality of our finitude and accommodate ourselves to it. If we pretend or imagine that life's purpose lies outside living itself, we will be searching the stars for what is underneath our feet all the time.

Hedonism

Earlier, when I gave an example of something that was worthwhile in itself, I talked about eating a good meal. That might suggest that what makes living worthwhile is nothing more complex than pleasure. Pleasure is, after all, a good thing in itself, something that, if we are experiencing it, does not need any further purpose to justify it. So, if life is finite and we need to find meaning in what is good in itself in life, surely we should just devote ourselves to pleasure?

Arguably, this is the secular orthodoxy of our day. Carpe diem—seize the day—has become the motto for our times. Encouraged by the media, in editorial and in advertising, we look for new and better pleasures all the time. If you were to spend just one day deliberately trying to spot how many articles in newspapers and magazines and advertisements in all media offer the promise of greater pleasure, you'll soon lose count. This is especially true if you read men's or women's lifestyle magazines, which seem solely to offer the promise of a happier, more contented, sexually stunning you. If any of these tips actually worked, people would soon

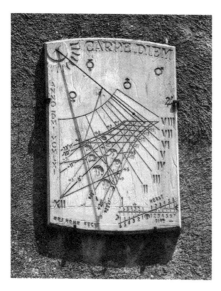

The phrase "Carpe diem," or seize the day, comes from an ode written by the Latin poet Horace in 23 BCE. The message often appears on sundials as a reminder that time passes swiftly and that we should enjoy every minute of every day. This sundial, created by René Rodolphe Joseph Rohr in 1961, is located in the old city of Carcassonne, France.

have no need to read these magazines. Yet their circulations remain stubbornly high. I think that tells us something.

What is also revealing is that we are widely reported to be in general a rather dissatisfied society. In developed Western countries, we have access to more and better sources of pleasure than our predecessors could imagine. Yet we are not a noticeably fulfilled bunch. What's gone wrong?

This apparent paradox would not surprise most of the great philosophers of ethics, all of whom have been suspicious of too great an emphasis on pleasure. The main problem, variously explained, is that pleasure is by its nature transitory. It is all very well feeling good but pleasure does not in general leave a very long-lasting afterglow. Indeed, a life devoted to pleasure can be hard work, since if one is really serious about it, then one has to make a constant effort to get more and more.

The present always eludes our grasp, so pleasures of the present are from the moment they are attained doomed to slip through our fingers.

This is why a life devoted to pleasure is for most of us deeply unsatisfying. Certainly a good life has its fair share of pleasure and only the most puritan of ethicists have claimed otherwise. But contentment or satisfaction requires more than just transitory pleasure. It requires us to be living the kind of lives that make us feel satisfied even when we are not particularly enjoying ourselves. There is no formula for determining what kind of life this is, and it certainly varies considerably from person

This advertisement for Wolcott's Instant Pain Annihilator, created around 1863, would certainly not conform to today's truth-in-advertising laws. It's an extreme example of what we are bombarded with daily—inducements to seek pleasure and comfort as ends in themselves.

Democritus (ca. 460 BCE–ca. 370 BCE), the Greek materialist philosopher, seems to be the earliest philosopher on record to have categorically embraced a hedonistic world view. He often appears in portraits laughing or smiling, supposedly at the follies of mankind.

to person. For some, a hedonistic life does provide ongoing satisfaction as well as transitory pleasure. For others, a quiet, slow labor of love that to an outsider may seem quite joyless can provide deep satisfaction.

The main point here is simply that we should not be too quick to assume that if this is the only life we've got, and if life's meaning is to be found in the living of life itself, then that means we should pursue a life of pleasure. That may fit the negative stereotype of the shallow atheist who seeks intoxication with pleasure to fill the emptiness of his purposeless life, but it is as accurate a view of typical atheists as the joyless Bible thumper is of the religious believer.

Death

I hope to have shown how life can have meaning and purpose for atheists. But what if we turn the question on its head: why should anyone think that life *can't* have meaning or purpose for atheists? Why does the meaning of life seem to pose a special problem for atheists?

The answer seems to be that the atheist, not believing in any supernatural realm, believes that death in this natural Earth is the end of life. The atheist unequivocally accepts human mortality, with no belief in afterlife, reincarnation, or even dissolution of the ego into the world spirit. So, it is thought, if life is short and death is final, what is the point of it all?

I have already provided some answers to this. What I haven't yet done is questioned why an acceptance of mortality seems to make life any less meaningful than a belief in the afterlife does. There can only be two explanations for this: one is that life needs to be longer than it actually is to be meaningful; the other is that life needs to be endless to be meaningful. Neither assumption survives scrutiny.

Take the idea that life can only have a meaning if it never ends. It is certainly not the case that in general only endless activities can be meaningful. Indeed, usually the contrary is true: there being some end or completion is often required for an activity to have any meaning. A football match, for example, gains its purpose only because it finishes after ninety minutes and there is a result. An endless football match would

Most works of literature, poetry, film, and any kind of human narrative require closure in order to be fully meaningful. *Notorious*, a 1946 thriller directed by Alfred Hitchcock and starring Cary Grant and Ingrid Bergman, is no different.

be as meaningless as a kick around in the park. Plays, novels, films, and other forms of narrative also require some kind of completion. When we study we follow courses that end at a determinate point and don't go on forever. Take virtually any human activity and you find that some kind of closure or completion is required to make them meaningful.

This line of thought can make us wonder whether life would actually be *less* meaningful if it were eternal. What would be the point of doing anything if we had an eternity to live? Why bother trying to do anything, such as improve your golf swing, if you've always got time to do it later? Isn't it rather that the knowledge of mortality, the sound of "time's winged chariot hurrying near," is what drives us and makes getting on with life meaningful at all?

It might be objected that eternal life would be meaningless if it were just more of the same, more of this life. But it would be meaningful if it were a different kind of life, perhaps an existence in some pure state of bliss or nirvana.

There are two problems with this view. The first is that if eternal life is not recognizably this kind of life then it is not clear how the person living it could be recognizably you or me. We are embodied human beings and our whole *modus operandi* is one of human beings with thoughts, feelings, plans, relationships, hungers, and disappointments. The life of a disembodied something, with no thought of past and future but just an eternal absorption in a feeling of bliss, seems to me to be nothing like my life at all. So we are faced with a dilemma. Either the afterlife is recognizably like this life, in which case an eternal one does not look very meaningful; or it is not like this life at all, in which case it doesn't look like the kind of life we could actually live.

The second problem with this view is that it is based on the idea that some states are worth being in for their own sake. The whole point about nirvana is that we do not need to ask what the point of being in that state is—it is simply valuable in itself. But if we accept that some forms of existence can be worth living for themselves, then why ignore the valuable form of life we actually have and instead hold out some hope for an idealized form of life to come?

So the idea that life needs to be eternal to be meaningful is simply false. What of the alternative suggestion that it needs to be much longer to be meaningful? This is very unpersuasive. If finite life can have meaning then it seems odd to think that it must be finite life of a certain length. Human life is, by the measure of the universe, a blink of an eye. Even in terms of our human perceptions, life can fly by distressingly quickly. Yet at the same time, for every person who reaches old age still hungry for life, there is another who has been worn out by life's ups and downs and is getting tired. Life may not be the perfect length, but it is long enough to be meaningful.

This cartoon, in which a man plays chess with the Grim Reaper, reminds us of life's finitude. It was created by the artist Walter Appleton Clark and appeared in the February 17, 1906, issue of *Collier's Weekly*, illustrating a piece by the ghost-story writer Georgia Wood Pangborn.

I personally do not go along with the view that life is just about the right length. The reason often cited for this is not the idea that nature has just made us lucky, but that we live our lives according to what is the norm, and that if the average lifespan were longer we wouldn't lead more meaningful lives, we would just adjust our life plans accordingly by, for instance, being in less of a hurry to establish ourselves in careers. This is a comforting thought, but I actually think it would be good if life could be somewhat longer than it usually is—provided those extra years could be lived in good health. There is so much to do that seventy or so years does seem a rather mean allotment. Accepting one's mortality is not the same as believing that this is the best of all possible worlds. Not only is our average lifespan on the short side, too many people do not even live that long.

As Othello regards Desdemona with a dagger in his hand near the end of Shakespeare's legendary drama *Othello*, we know that the scene's conclusion—like that of life itself—is inevitable. This poster was published in England in the 1920s.

Death thus occupies a crucial role in the atheist world view. It is the final full stop that makes life meaningful in the first place, but its coming too soon or even as early as it usually does can still be a cause of regret. There is some truth in the cliché that all good things must come to an end, but just as the curtain falling on Othello does not make the play worse, but is actually a necessary condition for it being any good in the first place, so we may regret death while at the same time knowing that its inevitability is what makes life so valuable in the first place.

Meaningful Lives

Although I have here argued the case for the possibility of meaningful atheist lives, perhaps it is more persuasive simply to point to the reality of such lives. Many atheists do and have lived meaningful and purposeful lives, and for others to deny this seems to be remarkably arrogant.

If you visit the Web site celebatheists.com, you will find a long list of living atheists. Among them is Arundhati Roy, award-winning author of *The God of Small Things* and a campaigner for social change and justice in India. In an interview, asked if she thought death was the end, she replied, "Yes . . . sometimes even before you die, that's it." I think this sharp reply shows how an atheist belief in mortality can motivate a real concern for those who, though still living, are not getting a good chance to enjoy the only life they have.

Interestingly, a lot of famous atheists are writers, thinkers, or artists. Milan Kundera, Czech author of *The Unbearable Lightness of Being*, is an atheist, while Terry Pratchett, author of the Discworld novels, says, "I think I'm probably an atheist, but rather angry with God for not existing."

Perhaps the biggest challenge to people who think atheists cannot live meaningful lives is the Czech Republic, where forty percent of the population is atheist. Take a holiday to Prague and see if you're overcome by a wave of meaninglessness.

History is also populated with a good number of atheists, including the former French president François Mitterrand (1916–96), American physicist Richard Feynman (1918–88), the father of modern Turkey Mustafa Kemal Ataturk (1881–1938), and Nobel Prize-winning chemist and physicist Marie Curie (1867–1934).

I am not saying that all of these people are heroes, or that we should admire all they did. Atheists live good and bad lives, just as do priests,

Forty percent of the population of the Czech Republic is atheist, but the vibrant cultural, intellectual, and economic life of its capital, Prague, proves that atheism need not be associated with a life of meaninglessness. This photograph, taken in 2005, shows some of the architecture for which the city is renowned.

The Nobel Prize–winning chemist and physicist Marie Sklodowska Curie, who appears in this undated photograph, is one of many well-known, high-achieving individuals who have professed their atheism.

popes, and rabbis. The point is simply that these are all lives lived with purpose and meaning, concrete proof that a life without belief in God is not a life without direction or significance. The greatest proof that something is possible is to show that it actually exists. These people show that meaningful atheist lives are more than theoretical possibilities. They are around us every day.

FIVE

Atheism in History

·

Not the History of Atheism

MY CONCERN IN THIS CHAPTER is to not present a potted history of atheism, for two reasons. The first is that the subject is just too vast for a short chapter, especially by a nonhistorian such as myself. The second relates to the overall aims of this book. I want to keep the focus on offering reasons to think atheism is true and arguing against reasons to think it is false, not to discuss everything to do with atheism.

My interest in the history of atheism is thus limited to two specific questions which, I think, need to be answered as part of my

The Greek historian Thucydides (ca. 460–ca. 395 BCE) is credited with pioneering a new kind of historical chronicle—one that relies on evidence and factual analysis rather than on mythologizing and narrative re-creation. Thucydides was also the first historian of his era to interpret events on their own terms rather than as consequences of divine intervention. This statue of Thucydides stands in front of the Austrian parliament building in Vienna. In the background, ironically, is the Athena Fountain, which pays homage to the Greek goddess of wisdom.

wider argument for atheism. The first of these is the question of when and why atheism emerged in Western history. The second concerns the extent to which atheism is implicated in the terrors of twentieth-century totalitarianism in the Soviet Union, Nazi Germany, Italy, and Spain. The answer to the first strengthens the case for atheism, while an answer to the second weakens some objections to it.

The Birth of Atheism

When did atheism begin? There are two answers to this question which may appear to be in conflict with one another. One is that atheism began at the dawn of Western civilization itself, in ancient Greece. James Thrower argues this case in his *Western Atheism*. The other is that atheism only fully emerged as late as the eighteenth century. This is what David Berman claims in his *A History of Atheism in Britain*. The conflict is, however, merely apparent, for there is a single story which is consistent with both Thrower's and Berman's accounts. This is that atheism had its origins in ancient Greece but did not emerge as an overt and avowed belief system until late in the Enlightenment.

Thrower's argument is based on the necessary connection between naturalism and atheism. As we saw in Chapter 1, atheism can be understood not simply as a denial of religion, but as a self-contained belief system, if it is seen as a commitment to the view that there is only one world and this is the world of nature.

If this is the right way to view atheism, and I agree with Thrower that it is, then to understand the origins of atheism you have to understand the origins of naturalism. And naturalism starts with the pre-Socratic Milesian philosophers of the sixth century BCE, Thales, Anaximander, and Anaximenes. These philosophers were the first to reject mythological explanations in favor of naturalistic ones. Whereas previously the origins and functions of the world were all explained by myths, the Milesians worked on the then revolutionary idea that nature could be understood as a self-contained system that operated according to laws that were comprehensible by human reason. This marked a fundamental shift in the orientation of explanatory accounts. No longer was it necessary to postulate anything outside of nature to understand how nature worked: the answers were all to be found within nature itself.

This therefore also marked the point where science began, although it would be a long time before it matured into what we would now recognize as rigorous experimental science. However, it would be a mistake to overemphasize the extent to which the pre-Socratic philosophers were specifically proto-scientists. Critics of atheism often argue that it is too in thrall to science, that it takes scientific explanation to be the only kind of legitimate explanation, and that therefore its

Thales, Anaximander, and Anaximenes, the Milesian philosophers—named for the ancient Anatolian town of Miletus, in present-day Turkey, from which they hailed—were the first thinkers of their time to reject mythological explanations for natural phenomena. This crudely hand-colored illustration of Thales (ca. 624–ca. 546 BCE), dressed anachronistically in Middle-Age garb, appeared in an early printed edition of the Nuremberg Chronicle, a fifteenth-century historical narrative.

rejection of religion is based on a too-narrow conception of what kinds of explanation are useful or even truthful. The account offered by Thrower of the origins of atheism might seem to reinforce this criticism, if the origins of atheism are identified with the origins of science.

This criticism is mistaken, however, because science is only one of the fruits of the new way of looking at the world initiated by the pre-Socratics. The revolution in thought they started was not the replacement of mythology by science in particular, but the replacement of myth by rational explanation in general.

To illustrate this, consider the development of history in Ancient Greece between the works of Herodotus and Thucydides, as discussed by Thrower and the philosopher Bernard Williams in his *Truth and Truthfulness*. Here we find another example of the rejection of myth in favor of something more rational. The real history of this development is not one of a switch being flicked between the wholly mythologizing Herodotus and the plain factuality of Thucydides. Nevertheless, an important boundary was crossed when Thucydides set out to discuss history as a series of factual and dated events which fit together to tell some kind of causal story. As Williams puts it, the histories of Thucydides aimed at "telling the truth" as it is. The view of history offered by Thucydides is now so commonsensical (though not to many academic historians) that it is difficult to imagine how people could ever have thought of history otherwise. This only underlines how radical a development Thucydides's history was.

There is a connection between the development of Milesian philosophy and Thucydidian history which is more than just the common rejection of myth. The connection is between what *replaces* myth. In both cases what usurps myth is rationality. A rational account is broadly one which confines itself to reasons, evidence and arguments that are open to scrutiny, assessment, acceptance, or rejection on the basis of principles and facts which are available to all. An optimally rational account is one in which we don't have to plug any gaps with speculation, opinion, or any other ungrounded beliefs.

In this sense, the science for which the pre-Socratics laid the foundations and the way of studying history begun by Thucydides are both characterized by their rational nature. History becomes the attempt to tell the story of the past based on evidence and arguments which are available to and assessable by all. Science becomes the attempt to give an account of the workings of the world based on evidence and arguments which are available to and assessable by all. This is the broader revolution in thought initiated by the Milesians.

In this sense we can see how the naturalism which lies at the heart and root of atheism is itself rooted in a

This statue of the Greek historian Herodotus (ca. 484–ca. 425 BCE) is located in the Library of Congress in Washington, D.C. Herodotus is known as the father of history because he was the first to systematically collect and arrange the results of his inquiries into a vivid narrative, albeit one colored by several personal observations and digressions—a technique that stands in stark contrast to the scientific approach of his successor Thucydides.

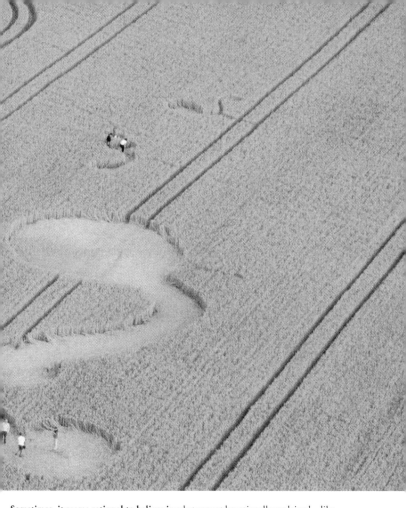

Sometimes, it seems rational to believe in what cannot be rationally explained—like consciousness. However, most atheists would argue that it's decidedly irrational to leap from an absence of a clear explanation to wild speculation as to the real causes of a phenomenon—like crop circles. This photograph, taken in August of 1997, shows investigators from the Crop Circle Research Project studying crop circles found in Wiltshire, England. The county of Wiltshire, where mysterious crop circles appear every summer, mostly in fields of standing corn, remains one of the most active areas for crop-circle sightings in the world.

broader commitment to rationalism. (This kind of rationalism-with-a-small-r is not to be confused with the seventeenth-century Rationalism-with-a-capital-R, which is much more specific and ambitious in the claims it makes for the power of rationality.) Naturalism follows from rationalism, and so it is rationalism, rather than naturalism, which is fundamental to the origins of atheism. So it is not the case that atheism follows merely from some shallow commitment to the primacy of scientific inquiry. It is rather that atheism is grounded in a wider commitment to the value of rational explanation, of which science is merely one spectacularly successful example.

It is sometimes objected that atheists are too committed to the value of rational explanation. This critique may be prima facie appealing if it is seen as advocating a world view which encompasses more than what can be rationally explained. But of course a rationalist can accept such a world view too, just as long as that means we only accept what cannot be rationally explained if we have rational reasons to suppose it exists. For example, many would agree that we do not have a rational explanation for how consciousness can be produced in physical brains, but there are rational reasons to suppose consciousness exists because we are all conscious beings. In this sense it is rational to believe in the existence of what cannot yet be rationally explained. But in the case of, say, ghosts, we not only lack a rational explanation of how ghosts can exist, we also lack any rational reasons to suppose that they do.

So to make the criticism of atheist rationalism do any work, it has to be claimed that atheists are wrong to say we should not believe in anything we have no rational reason to think exists. It is hard to see how anyone could argue this line without opening the door to any number of irrational absurdities. For example, if you want to seriously argue that we should believe in things we have no rational reason to think exist, why not believe in the tooth fairy? (Non-atheists tend to get irritated when atheists invoke entities such as the tooth fairy and Santa Claus to illustrate the ridiculousness of permitting belief in what is not rational, but such irritation does not comprise a serious counterargument.)

Of course, intelligent non-atheists have more to say on this point, as do atheists in response. There is no space to pursue the argument further here, for my point has already been made. In short, atheism is rooted in naturalism, which is itself rooted in rationalism. The origins of both rationalism and naturalism are to be found in ancient Greece and so in an important sense this marks the first chapter in the history of atheism. What is so significant about this is that an identification has been made between the origins of atheism and the origins of Western rationality as

The Declaration of the Rights of Man and Citizen is a fundamental document of the French Revolution. Its principles were heavily influenced by the political philosophy of the Enlightenment, which advanced the notion that the powers of the church and state should be separate. A reproduction of the declaration—pointedly pictured on two stone tablets, echoing the iconography of the Ten Commandments—appears in this 1789 painting by the artist Jean Jacques Francois LeBarbier.

a whole. Thus atheism can be seen as part of a wider, progressive story about the development of human intellect and understanding. This identification of atheism and progress is reinforced when one considers the next major stage in atheism's development: the Enlightenment.

The Birth of Avowed Atheism

In his history of atheism, David Berman is struck by how late atheism emerged as an avowed belief system. He claims the first avowedly atheist work was Baron d'Holbach's *The System of Nature*, published in 1770, while the first such work to be published in Britain was the *Answer to*

BARON D'HOLBACH

Paul-Henri Thiry, baron d'Holbach (1723–1789), was the first self-professed atheist in Europe. The wealthy French-German nobleman was a contributor to the Encyclopédie compiled by Denis Diderot (see page 120), and held a well-known and well-attended salon at his home in Paris, whose guests included the philosopher David Hume.

Dr. Priestley's letters to a philosophical unbeliever, published in 1782. The authorship of this latter text is disputed, and it is possible that it was the work of two men, William Hammon and Matthew Turner.

It is a matter of scholarly dispute whether or not any atheist works predate these. Thrower is certainly convinced that some writings of Democritus and Lucretius are atheistic, although he agrees that d'Holbach was the "first unequivocally professed atheist in the Western Tradition." So Thrower's general account is consistent with Berman's assertion that atheism did not emerge as a fully articulated distinctive force until the late eighteenth century. Before that we had isolated works that could be viewed as atheist, and even periods in history when God or the gods were seen as irrelevant in at least some sectors of society, such as among the upper classes of the early Roman Empire. But there was no systematic and ongoing attempt to present and promulgate a godless world view as an alternative to the religious one.

The story of how atheism emerged and established itself from this point on is an interesting one, which Berman dissects in detail. For our purposes, however, I just want to highlight two interesting features.

The first is that the emergence of atheism at this time fits in with the progressive story of atheism that sees its roots in the birth of Western rationality in Ancient Greece. Just as naturalism and rationalism, atheism's forebears, were the fruits of the progression from myth to reason, so atheism as an avowed doctrine is the fruit of the progression to Enlightenment values.

Although it has become fashionable to debunk the ideals of the Enlightenment, it is a mark of its success that its most basic doctrines are now fundamental to our conception of a civilized, modern society. We may debate the precise meaning of equality, liberty, and tolerance, but all three are central to our notion of what makes a good and fair society. We may have lost some of the Enlightenment's optimism in the power of reason, but we would certainly not like to go back to a society based on superstition. And although some may think that we have gone too far in our disrespect of authority, few seriously believe that we should go back to a time when office was inherited, when only the male middle classes were politically enfranchised, or when leading clerics wielded strong political power. So despite its faults, the Enlightenment has to be seen by any reasonable person as an important stage in the progression of Western society, and its core ideals have triumphed.

It would be too strong a claim to say that, because avowed atheism emerged riding on the back of the Enlightenment, that it must share in its glory. But it would be equally foolish to see the simultaneous emergence of modern atheism and the Enlightenment as purely coincidental. Their arrival at the same point in history is at least suggestive of a connection, and it is not hard to see how that connection might be made. Atheism takes the Enlightenment rejection of superstition, hierarchy, and rationally ungrounded authority to what many would see as its logical conclusion. It certainly fits atheism's self-image to say that, once we were prepared to look religion in the eye under the cool light of reason, its untruth became self-evident. It just obviously was superstition and myth, grounded not in the divine but in particular, local human practices. On this view, it is impossible to take Enlightenment ideals seriously and cling on to the belief that religion represents truth.

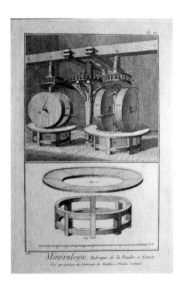

The French philosopher Denis Diderot (1713–84) is perhaps best known as the editor of *Encyclopédie, ou dictionnaire raisonné des sciences, des arts et des métiers* (*Encyclopedia, or a Systematic Dictionary of the Sciences, Arts, and Crafts*), published between 1751 and 1772. The massive thirty-five-volume work was an important exposition of Enlightenment ideals. This page from the Encyclopédie illustrates one phase of the process involved in making gunpowder.

So although I have not been able to make a watertight case for the claim here, it is certainly more than possible to explain the emergence of avowed atheism in the late Enlightenment in terms of a story of the ongoing progress of human society and intellect, even if that progress is uneven and reversible.

The second interesting point to note about the late emergence of avowed atheism is what it says about the deep embeddedness of religion in our society. One of the most fascinating features of Berman's account is how writers in the seventeenth century often denied even the possibility that anyone could ever be a genuine atheist—someone who really believed there was no God as opposed to someone who just acted as if God did not exist. Religion was just assumed to be universal. One could no more believe someone who denied the existence of God than one could deny the existence of the sun or stars.

Indeed, some used the supposed universal belief in God as an argument for God's existence. This variation on the old adage "Fifty million Frenchmen can't be wrong" strikes one as rather weak for a rational argument. After all, at one time nearly the whole world's population thought that rain came from the gods or that the earth was the center of the universe. They were, of course, wrong and it doesn't take much reflection to realize that widespread agreement cannot make something true or false. If it could, then we would not need to spend any time, say, searching for a cure for cancer. We could just all agree that eating chocolate does the trick.

What widespread belief in religion does show, however, is how atheism really has been battling against the odds. It also explains the historical reason why atheism has been defined negatively as the denial of belief in God, rather than positively as some kind of naturalism. As my

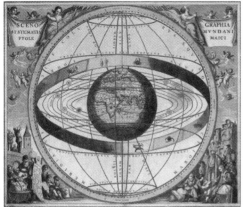

Many atheists point to the fact that most of humanity once subscribed to the geocentric theory as evidence that "fifty million Frenchmen" *can* be wrong. This illustration of the Ptolemaic conception of the universe comes from *Harmonia Macrocosmica* by Andreas Cellarius, a celestial atlas published in 1660.

Loch Ness story showed, one needs only to see atheism negatively in a context where religious belief is the norm. And religious belief has been, and still usually is, the norm the world over.

For a belief system to establish itself as a credible alternative to religion, believed by millions of people—especially, it has to be said, intelligent or educated people—contrary to almost unanimous opposition and in a little over two hundred years, is something of a triumph. But it is also a reminder of how little experience we have of living our lives and ordering our societies without the backdrop of religion. Mass atheism is young and as such we must expect to see some signs of its immaturity. Some of these, it is thought, may have been at least partly responsible for some of the last century's worst episodes. It is to these that we must now turn.

Atheism and Twentieth-Century Totalitarianism

One of the most serious charges laid against atheism is that it is responsible for some of the worst horrors of the twentieth century, including the Nazi concentration camps and Stalin's gulags. The godless regimes of fascism and communism could only commit such atrocities because they were godless. How should atheists respond to this charge?

One problem in answering these questions is that some of the history is contested. In particular, the deep causes of the Holocaust are the subject of fierce debate. This is not the place to settle such debates. So I shall try to base my arguments on what is generally agreed, using what is contested only as a means to show that some anti-atheist assumptions are just that—assumptions and not facts. In keeping with the style of this book, I shall not provide references and sources for all my claims in the text, but the information is there in the further reading section at the end of the book.

If we consider fascism first, the first obvious fact is that the role of religion in fascism varied enormously and is sometimes difficult to interpret. In Spain, the Catholic Church was on the side of the fascist Franco in the Civil War and continued to support him for many years after he came to power, with serious dissent of any kind not emerging until the 1960s. Indeed, many saw the Civil War as a kind of religious crusade against the godless republicans. There is still a great deal of controversy concerning the extent to which members of the Catholic prelature Opus Dei occupied positions of power in Franco's Spain.

The Spanish Civil War (1936–39) began with a coup d'etat staged by a group of generals against the elected (and anticlerical) left-wing government in power at the time. The war ended with the victory of the rebel troops and the founding of a dictatorship led by General Francisco Franco, which lasted until his death in 1975. Franco appears above in his officially sanctioned photographic portrait.

It is certainly true that Franco's Spain was not the most brutal of fascist regimes, but this is only by comparison with the extremes of Hitler. Consider Franco's repression and terrorizing of the Basques, for example, immortalized in Picasso's depiction of the bombing of Guernica at the busiest time on market day when maximum civilian casualties were assured. This was not atheist fascism but an expressly Catholic one.

In Italy too, the Vatican signed the notorious Lateran treaty with the fascist government in 1929, providing mutual recognition of fascist Italy and the Vatican State and making Mussolini the leader under whom Roman Catholicism became the official religion of Italy. Resistance to Mussolini grew throughout the 1930s, but at no time was there a clear majority in the Catholic Church opposed to his regime, even after 1938 when anti-Jewish laws were passed. So again it is hard to see how atheism can be seen to be the driving force behind Italian fascism.

The case of Nazi Germany is the most important one, for it was under Hitler that the worst fascist atrocities took place. But what is clear is that

There are those who consider atheism responsible for the atrocities that took place under the dictators Adolf Hitler and Benito Mussolini. On the contrary, however, neither of these regimes was atheist in theory or in practice. This photograph shows Hitler and Mussolini during Hitler's visit to Venice, Italy, in June of 1934.

in no way was Nazi Germany a straightforwardly atheist state. Hitler, for instance, maintained the traditional German view of women as needing to focus on "Kirche, Küche, Kinder"—church, kitchen, and children.

More substantively, a concordat was signed between the Nazi government and the Catholic Church in 1933. The collusion between the Protestant churches and the Nazi regime was even closer, helped by an anti-Semitic tradition in German Protestantism. Resistance came not from the established Protestant churches but by the breakaway Confessional Church, led by pastors Martin Niemöller and Dietrich Bonhoeffer. These dissidents are justifiably held up by Christians today as shining examples of principled resistance to Nazism, but the fact that they had to leave the established Church to lead this resistance is no cause for Christian celebration.

Nazi doctrines themselves were also at odds with the kind of rational naturalism of traditional atheism. Rather, Nazi ideology involved what historian Emilio Gentile calls the "sacralization of politics":

> This process takes place when, more or less elaborately and dogmatically, a political movement confers a sacred status on an earthly entity (the nation, the country, the state, humanity, society, race, proletariat, history, liberty, or revolution) and renders it an absolute principle of collective existence, considers it the main source of values for individual and mass behavior, and exalts it as the supreme ethical precept of public life. It thus becomes an object for veneration and dedication, even to the point of self-sacrifice.

> Translated by Robert Mallet from *Le religioni della politica. Fra democrazie e totalitarismi* (Roma Bari, Laterza, 2001)

Looked at in this context, the problem with Nazi Germany was not its supposed atheism but its elevation of concepts such as blood, soil, and nation to quasi-religious status. It should be clear from what has been said in this book that such sacralization is utterly foreign to mainstream rational atheism.

The last point I wish to mention with regard to Nazi Germany is that, complex though the causes of the Holocaust are, it seems impossible to deny the role played by religion in Western anti-Semitism. As historian Kristen Renwick Monroe writes:

> Religion played an integral part in the Holocaust. Christian churches from the time of Constantine in the fourth century had wanted to convert Jews, and medieval Christian churches throughout Europe engaged in varying degrees of persecution because they felt it was the Jews who had crucified Christ. This belief formed the basic foundation for anti-Semitism and was never contradicted, or even addressed directly, by any religious group throughout this period.

"Holocaust" in the *Encyclopedia of Politics and Religion*
(London, Routledge, 1998), p. 338

It does seem undeniable that the history of Christian anti-Semitism is at least partly to blame for creating the mindset within which the Holocaust could even be conceivable.

A more general point is that religion in general has tended to operate by setting up dichotomies between the righteous and the unrighteous, the saved and the damned, good peoples and bad ones. In this sense religion is by its nature not only divisive, but divisive in a way which elevates some people above others. It is not too fanciful, I think, to see how the centuries of religious tradition in Western society made possible the kind of distinction between the superior Aryans and the inferior others which Nazism required.

The idea that atheism was therefore the driving force of European fascism does not therefore seem at all persuasive. On the contrary, it seems to me at least that religion is probably more responsible for its horrors than atheism. However, it is not essential to my defense of atheism

The anti-Semitism that culminated in the Holocaust had been prevalent in Europe for generations, and some atheists point to its roots in religious belief. One of the most poignant horrors of the Holocaust was the failure of the Warsaw Ghetto Uprising, which took place between January and May of 1943, when the Jews confined to the Warsaw ghetto in Nazi-occupied Poland rebelled against the attempt to deport them to the concentration camp at Treblinka. This famous photograph was taken during the uprising.

that the blame is instead taken by religion. It is enough to show that there is nothing particularly atheist about fascist ideology or practice, and that therefore it is just wrong to blame atheism for its terrors.

Things are rather different when it comes to Soviet communism (and indeed Chinese and Asian communism, which I will not discuss here). Here, there is no question that we had an avowedly and officially atheist state. We also saw, under Stalin's rule in particular, mass extermination on a horrific scale. Does that mean atheism should be blamed for the disasters of state communism?

The fact that the Soviet Union was atheist is no more reason to think that atheism is necessarily evil than the fact that Hitler was a vegetarian is a reason to suppose that all vegetarians are Nazis. It is certainly a historical refutation of the idea that atheism must always be benign, but it is a very naïve atheist who thinks that it is impossible for atheists ever to do wrong. Christian critics who also think that the Soviet Union provides some kind of refutation of atheism would, by their own logic, have to accept that atrocities such as the crusades or inquisitions refute Christianity.

If the history of the Soviet Union is to be used in a case against atheism, it therefore has to be shown that it was somehow an inevitable or logical consequence of atheist beliefs. However, this is simply not plausible. The mere existence of millions of humane atheists in Western democracies who have no truck with state communism shows that there is no essential link between being an atheist and condoning the gulags.

However, there is I believe a salutary lesson to be learned from the way in which atheism formed an essential part of Soviet communism, even though Soviet communism does not form any essential part of atheism. This lesson concerns what can happen when atheism becomes too militant and Enlightenment ideals too optimistic.

Great Stalin - a symbol of friendship of nations of the USSR!

Beloved Stalin - the people's happiness!

The fact that the Soviet Union was an avowedly atheist state doesn't mean that atheism can be blamed for the mass murders committed by the communist dictator Joseph Stalin. The captions at the bottom of these propaganda posters are translations from the original Russian, but they accurately convey some of the efforts at concealing the truth of what went on during his tenure in power (1922–53).

Soviet communism had its intellectual roots in the communist philosophy of Karl Marx. Marx is well known for his adage that religion is "the opium of the people." But it is a mistake to take this phrase in isolation and suppose that Marx therefore thought religion needed to be abolished by force as soon as possible. Marx did believe in the abolition of religion, but the means of doing this would be to create a society in which the people no longer needed its consolations. There would be no need to ban religion since in a communist state it would simply become unnecessary.

So, we can see how Soviet communism is already two steps removed from the central beliefs of atheism. First, communism is just one atheist belief, and certainly not the most popular one. Second, Soviet communism, with its active oppression of religion, is a distortion of original Marxist communism, which did not advocate oppression of the religious.

In fact, even though it was officially atheist, it is not even true to say that the Soviet Union and the Church always had an antagonistic relationship. Stalin permitted the formation of the Moscow Patriarchate, a central body for the Russian Orthodox Church. According to historian Michael Bordeaux, throughout the years of Soviet rule, the Patriarchate

> overtly backed every military initiative of the Soviet regime: suppression of the Hungarian uprising (1956), the erection of the Berlin Wall (1961), the invasion of Czechoslovakia (1968) and Afghanistan (1979).

> "Russia" in the *Encyclopedia of Politics and Religion* (London, Routledge, 1998), p. 657

In the introduction to his 1843 work *Critique of Hegel's Philosophy of Right*, Karl Marx said: "Religion is, indeed, the self-consciousness and self-esteem of man who has either not yet won through to himself, or has already lost himself again . . . Religion is the sigh of the oppressed creature, the heart of a heartless world, and the soul of soulless conditions. It is the opium of the people." Marx is shown here in an undated wood engraving.

Post-Soviet claims that the Church had opposed the Soviet regime all along just don't wash.

So atheists can consistently distance themselves from the terrors of Stalin by simply pointing out that Soviet communism is not even a logical extension of Marxist communism, let alone a logical extension of core atheist values, which are not communist at all. However, although this defense is certainly enough to justify a "not guilty" verdict in the court of history, the Soviet experience does point to two dangers of atheism. The first of these is a too-zealous militancy. It is one thing to disagree with religion and quite another to think that the best way to counter it is by oppression and making atheism the official state credo. What happened in Soviet Russia is one of the reasons why I personally dislike militant atheism. When I heard someone recently say that they really thought religious belief was some kind of mental illness and that they looked forward to a time in the future when religious believers would be treated, I could see an example of how militant atheism can lead to totalitarian oppression. But this is not a danger specific to atheism. Fundamentalism is a danger in any belief system, and that is why I think the main danger we need to guard against is not religion but fundamentalism of any description.

Atheism's model should not thus be Soviet-style state atheism but Western-style state secularism. Indeed, secularism has been one of the great triumphs of Western civilization and one of the proudest legacies of the Enlightenment. The overwhelming majority of atheists do not want to see an atheist state but a secular one, in which matters of religion and belief are not regulated by government but left to individual conscience, in line with the broadly liberal tradition of individual liberty. The state should only intervene in religious matters to counter extremism which threatens the liberty of its citizens.

The second danger Soviet communism warns us against is the belief that society can be ordered by rational principles without regard to its traditions and history or a respect for the liberty of the individual.

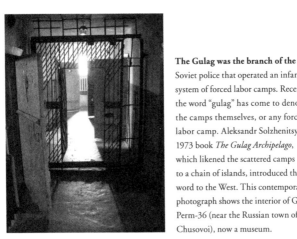

The Gulag was the branch of the Soviet police that operated an infamous system of forced labor camps. Recently, the word "gulag" has come to denote the camps themselves, or any forced labor camp. Aleksandr Solzhenitsyn's 1973 book *The Gulag Archipelago*, which likened the scattered camps to a chain of islands, introduced the word to the West. This contemporary photograph shows the interior of Gulag Perm-36 (near the Russian town of Chusovoi), now a museum.

It should be remembered that many Western intellectuals, including atheist freethinkers like Bertrand Russell, were originally very optimistic about the Soviet revolution. There was a naïve belief that it was possible to wipe the slate of society clean and start again following only rational principles of what is fair, just, and efficient. This wholesale disregard or denial of the importance of human nature and cultural traditions is partly responsible for the terrors that followed.

It is not at all necessary for atheists to go along with this belief and, indeed, hardly anyone now accepts it after having seen its consequences in the last century. Nevertheless, there is a danger in rational atheism of overestimating the extent to which things could be better if only we ordered society more rationally. If this means imposing a "more rational system" on an unwilling populace, the results will be catastrophic.

Conclusion

There are, I think, several interesting insights into atheism which can be gleaned by looking at its history. The first is that the rise of atheism is essentially linked to the emergence of rationalism in Ancient Greece and its subsequent march forward in the Enlightenment. Atheism is thus part of a progressive story of human culture in which superstition is replaced with rational explanation and in which we lose the illusions of the supernatural realm and come to learn how to live within the natural one.

The second is the negative point that atheism is not to be blamed for the terrors of twentieth-century totalitarianism. There is, however, a need to remember that militant or fundamentalist atheism, which seeks to overturn religious belief by force, is as dangerous as any other form of fundamentalism. Atheism's most authentic political expression thus takes the form of state secularism, not state atheism.

SIX

Against Religion?

•

Wrong and Bad

THERE IS A PERCEPTION OF ATHEISTS that their main concern is to attack religion. This is part of the wider perception of atheism as being essentially antireligious in character, rather than pro-naturalist. This perception is hard to shift, because in most countries of the world, religions get more respect than atheism, and thus atheists find themselves fighting their corner and being seen as troublesome enemies of religion in the process.

One recent incident in the United Kingdom illustrates how easy it is for the wrong impression to be made. There is a long-running

A member of the NoToPope coalition wears a T-shirt during a fashion show held outside the New South Wales state parliament in Australia on July 9, 2008, to protest Pope Benedict XVI's visit to Sydney. Demonstrations like these promote the view of atheism as antireligion rather than pro-naturalism.

three-minute slot on the most important morning radio news program in the country called "Thought for the Day." In an otherwise secular program, this allows spokespeople from a number of religions to offer a supposedly edifying, though more often than not trite, homily. The three main atheist membership organizations in the country, the British Humanist Association, the National Secular Society, and the Rationalist Press Association, have long campaigned to allow nonreligious viewpoints in the slot. The point is not that they want the religious viewpoints removed. It is rather that they are justifiably irritated at being excluded and angry that this reinforces the message that only religions can speak with authority on matters of ethics and life guidance.

However, when a letter protesting about the exclusion of atheists signed by many prominent people in public life received news coverage, many perceived the whole campaign as atheists engaging in a petty attack on the religious. (It did not help that the BBC commissioned a one-off alternative thought for the day from a vociferous opponent of religion whom they must have known would, and perhaps encouraged to, take the opportunity to be hostile.) Just as many feminists who want only equal representation for women have been lazily caricatured as "man-haters," so atheists who object to the religious monopoly on values education are labeled "antireligious."

Atheists are *necessarily* antireligious in one sense only: they believe that religions are false. But in this sense of the word "anti" most Muslims are anti-Christian, most Christians anti-Jewish, most Protestants anti-Roman Catholic, and so on. We would be wise, however, not to start calling all of these groups anti-whatever just because they disagree. To set any group up as "anti" another suggests more than disagreement, it

This photograph shows Karen Watts and Martin Reijns, who got married at the Royal Zoological Gardens in Edinburgh, Scotland, on June 18, 2005. The ceremony was notable for the fact that it was the UK's first legally sanctioned humanist marriage. In the past, nonreligious weddings have required a second, civil ceremony to be legal. But recent laws introduced in Scotland mean that nonreligious weddings can take place without a minister or civil registrar present. Such laws are a positive step toward allowing theists and atheists to coexist without conflict in society.

suggests hostility, and atheists are no more required to be hostile to the religious than Jews are required to be hostile to Hindus.

Of course, there are antireligious atheists, just as there are in fact anti-Protestant Catholics and vice versa. I will look at some of the reasons for adopting such a hostile attitude later. But such hostility is neither inevitable nor required by atheism.

Atheist opposition to religion is thus essentially an opposition to its truth. So it is necessary for any defense of atheism to address the challenge posed by religious belief. After all, many intelligent people are religious and it is not good enough for atheists to simply dismiss religious belief as foolish superstition. I have so far shown how strong the case is for atheism. To complete the argument, however, it is necessary to consider the merits of the major alternative.

Arguments for God's Existence

Pick up any introduction to the philosophy of religion and you'll see a number of traditional arguments for the existence of God. Great sport can be had showing why these arguments fail, but to my mind it is not worth spending too much time on them for the simple reason that these arguments don't provide the reasons why people become religious. This isn't just my view, but the honest opinion of many religious people who give much thought to the arguments. For instance, Peter Vardy, a Christian philosopher and author of several leading textbooks in the philosophy of religion which consider these arguments, calls them "a waste of time." Russell Stannard, the leading physicist who wrote a book called *The God Experiment* on evidence for God's existence, says, "I don't have to believe in God, I *know* that God exists—that is how I feel." In other words, evidence and arguments are neither here nor there—it is personal conviction that really counts.

What then is the true function of the so-called arguments for God's existence? Vardy's explanation of Aquinas's intentions in formulating his versions of the argument seems to offer the best explanation. "I think what he was trying to do was to show everybody who believed—and after all, everybody did—that belief was rational," he says. "I'm not at all sure he would have conceived it as a stand-alone proof."

Vardy is basically defining a form of argument called apologetics. The function of such arguments is not to show that God exists, but to show that belief in God does not require any irrationality. It is about reconciling belief and reason, not showing belief to be justified through reason. To see the difference, consider this analogy. A groom-to-be wakes up on his wedding morning to find his fiancée has

Saint Thomas Aquinas, shown here in this detail from an altarpiece in Ascoli Piceno, Italy, was one of the first apologists of Christian theology. His arguments for the existence of God were an effort to show believers that their belief was rational.

disappeared without a trace. He believes without adequate rational justification that she has gone to South America to reunite with a former lover. He thus lacks rational grounds for his belief, but that does not mean that his view is necessarily contrary to reason either. As long as his belief is consistent with the evidence, it can be reconciled to reason, if not justified by it.

I think that the traditional arguments for God's existence work in the same way. They do not prove that God exists. At best they can show that belief in God's existence is consistent with reason and evidence. They aim to show that God's existence is neither contrary to nor supported by reason, but compatible with it, just as the groom's belief is compatible with the evidence, but no more.

What then are these arguments? I do not wish to spend too much time on them, but it is worth at least sketching out their general form and showing their inadequacies, if only because versions of them are sometimes wheeled out by religious believers to challenge the atheist.

The Cosmological Argument

The cosmological argument in a nutshell is that since everything must have a cause, the universe must have a cause. And the only cause of the universe that could be up to the job is God, or at least that the best hypothesis for the cause of the universe is God. The cosmological

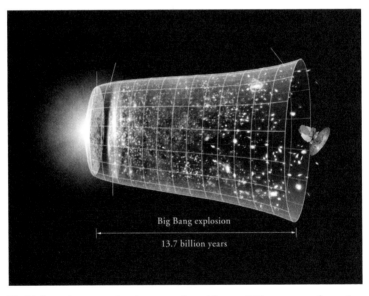

Big Bang explosion

13.7 billion years

The big bang theory says that, between twelve and fourteen billion years ago, the portion of the universe we can see today was only a few millimeters across. It has since expanded from this hot dense state into the vast and much cooler cosmos we currently inhabit. The theory also holds that the universe continues to expand to this day. The big bang is a focal point for discussion between atheists and those who believe that the universe was created by God. This image, generated by NASA, is a graphic representation of the history of the universe from its conception until the present.

argument is there whenever someone turns around and says to the naturalist, "Ah, well the universe may have begun with the big bang, but what caused the big bang?"

The argument is to my mind utterly awful, a disgrace to the good name of philosophy and the only reason for discussing it is to expose sloppy thinking. One fatal flaw among many is that the argument is based on principles it then flouts. The intuitive principles that lie behind the argument are that nothing exists uncaused and that the cause of something great and complex must itself be even greater and more complex. But it ends by hypothesizing God's existence as simple and uncaused. If it is possible for God to exist without a cause greater than God, why can't the universe exist without a cause greater than itself? Either the principles that inform the argument stand or they don't. If they stand, then God requires a cause and the causal chain goes back *ad infinitum*. If they don't, then there is no need to hypothesize God.

The second fatal flaw is that even if the logic of the argument works, we do not arrive at God. What we arrive at is a cause which is greater and more complex than the universe itself and which is itself uncaused. Whether or not this resembles the traditional God, who is much more like an individual personality than a super-universe, is surely open to question. So the argument cannot really establish that the cause is anything like God at all.

Viewed as an example of apologetics, however, we can see the true merits of the argument. It shows how it is possible for the religious to reconcile their beliefs with what we know about the universe. It is compatible with reason and what we know to suppose that the big bang was caused by God, and it is possible that all things within the universe must have a cause but that the causal chain, since it must stop somewhere, stops with God. So just as long as believers do not mistake the argument as evidence for God's existence, they can maintain the argument as a demonstration of the *rational possibility* of their belief in God. This leaves open the question of what really *justifies* belief in God, which we will come to shortly.

One further caution is that this kind of argument is precarious as it essentially hypothesizes a "God of the gaps." God is invoked to explain what we cannot currently explain. This is a risky strategy. After all, people previously invoked God to explain all sorts of natural phenomena we later explained, and each time God had to retreat further back into the unknown. In this case God has retreated to behind the blue touch-paper that started the universe going. Such a God is fast running out of places for believers to hide him.

The Teleological Argument

This is another terrible argument that compares the universe to a mechanism such as a watch. If you find a watch you have to suppose that there was a watchmaker. Such a complex, intricate mechanism could not have come into existence by pure chance. Now consider the universe: it is even more intricate and complex and so there is even more reason to suppose it did not come into existence by chance. Therefore, there must be some great architect or designer behind it: God.

The analogy fails because the universe just isn't a mechanism like a watch. When we see a rabbit, for example, we do not look for a rabbit-maker. We think instead it had parents. Unlike artifacts, objects in the natural world emerge through natural processes, processes which are pretty well understood. Read a book like Richard Dawkins's *The Blind Watchmaker*, for example, and you can see how evolution accounts for the

Many religious people, past and present, envision God as the "great artificer of all that moves," in the words of the poet William Cowper—a kind of technician or geometer who works behind the scenes. That belief gives rise to images like this one, a woodcut by the artist Julius Schnorr von Carolsfeld from an 1860 Bible, which depicts God separating day from night on the fourth day of creation.

appearance of design we find. Indeed, if you look at what we do know about how universes form and organisms grow, the hand of any designer is conspicuous only by its absence.

Furthermore, as David Hume pointed out, we can only hypothesize a watchmaker because we know by experience what the cause of watches are. We have no such experience of causes of the universe, so we are not justified in making any assumptions about who or what they might be. We might add that it seems terribly anthropocentric to suppose that the creator of the universe is some kind of deluxe personality, an omnipotent, omnibenevolent, and omniscient version of ourselves. Why shouldn't it be something more abstract, not recognizable as the traditional God of religion at all?

So once again the argument fails spectacularly to establish God's existence, but it does provide room for God. It is not contrary to reason and evidence to believe that there is an intelligent mind behind all this. But that is not to say there are positive reasons to believe that there is. Those reasons are still elusive.

The Ontological Argument

The ontological argument is at least philosophically interesting, but it is not more successful. Indeed, in some ways it is the weakest of the three arguments because it doesn't even contribute to apologetics.

There are many versions of the ontological argument. What they all have in common is that they attempt to show there is some kind of logical contradiction generated if we suppose that God does not exist, and that therefore God by logical necessity must exist.

One way of doing this is to think of the concept of God and to recognize that such a concept is of a supremely perfect entity. Now a perfect entity that did not exist is clearly not supremely perfect, since an entity which is the same but existent would be superior. So the concept of a supremely perfect entity must be a concept of an existing entity, and therefore by examining the concept of God alone we can see that God must exist by pain of contradiction.

The way I have summarized this argument makes its flaw clear: all we can show by logic is that the *concept* of God includes the *concept* of existence. But these are merely truths about concepts. We cannot, however, move from such truths about concepts to reach conclusions about what exists in the real world. For example, the concept of a circle is clearly defined by mathematical formulae, but we cannot conclude from the concept of a circle that any actual circles that meet the strict mathematical formulation exist in the real world, or even that real space conforms to the rules of Euclidean geometry within which circles are defined.

There is another way in which we can see how the ontological argument goes awry. The argument works by showing a supposed logical incompatibility between God and nonexistence. This is analogous to other pairs of concepts that logically require each other. Descartes talked about mountains and valleys, for example. There is a similar dependence of the concepts of wife and husband. What this logical dependence shows is that a wife without a husband cannot exist (as a wife that is—the woman who is the wife could exist without a husband, it's just that she would no longer be a wife). Continue the analogy with God and existence and you do not get the stunning conclusion that God must exist, but the banal truth that a God without existence could not exist. This does not mean that God must exist, but that *if* God exists, God must exist.

Many volumes have been written about the ontological argument, but most philosophers would now agree that it makes the mistake of leaping from truths about concepts to truths about existence, a leap

The French philosopher René Descartes (1596–1650) wrote a well-known meditation on the question of God's existence, in which he said: "I cannot conceive a God unless as existing, any more than I can a mountain without a valley, yet, just as it does not follow that there is any mountain in the world merely because I conceive a mountain with a valley, so likewise, though I conceive God as existing, it does not seem to follow on that account that God exists; for my thought imposes no necessity on things." This undated engraving of Descartes was modeled after a painting by Franz Hals.

which is not logical. The argument thus joins the teleological and the cosmological in the philosophical filing cabinet marked "past mistakes to be learned from."

What Then Justifies Belief?

I am sure that most religious believers will not be too concerned to see these arguments get short shrift because very few, if any, religious believers were persuaded to adopt their faith on the basis of them. But if arguments like these cannot justify belief, what can? As a matter of fact, it seems that most religious believers justify their faith by an inner conviction. As Russell Stannard said, for the believer, it is as though they know God exists and no further arguments are required. The leading Christian philosopher of religion Alvin Plantinga calls this faith, understood as "a special source of knowledge, knowledge that can't be arrived at by way of reason alone."

I think it's important that believers and nonbelievers recognize this. If this is indeed the ground of religious belief, then it is disingenuous for believers to put forward arguments to support their beliefs. Similarly, it is futile for atheists to attack the religious with arguments undermining these reasons for belief if they are not genuine reasons for belief at all.

Grounding religious belief in this kind of conviction, which feels to the believer like the direct apprehension of absolute truth, can utterly negate the power of all the arguments for atheism I have advanced so far. We can compare this to the force of argument against the existence of the self. Descartes famously said that the one thing he could not doubt was the existence of his own self. Many would agree with him, with the consequence that no rational argument against the existence of the self could shake the basic conviction we have of our own existence. Skepticism dissolves when confronted with the phenomenological certainty—the indubitable feeling—of our own existence. For many religious believers, their belief in God's existence is of comparable strength. They feel the truth of God's existence so strongly that they can no more doubt it than they can doubt the existence of their own selves.

I personally have little interest in trying to destroy these convictions, except when the holding of them leads to unpleasant and bigoted actions and proclamations, as can be the case with fundamentalist believers of all religions. I would, however, say two things about this which are of interest to believers who are prepared to at least question their convictions and to atheists striving to understand religious belief.

The first is that we should be very careful about what we say cannot be doubted. "Cannot be doubted" can really mean "don't want to doubt" or "cannot imagine the thing being doubted not being true." It may seem to the religious that they can no more doubt God's existence than their own, but this cannot be universally true, since plenty of people lose their belief in God and yet no psychologically healthy person loses her belief in herself (although plenty, after philosophical reflection, lose their belief in what they thought the self was). To those who say they cannot imagine the possibility of God not existing, I say try a little harder. Imagine what it is like for atheists. You must be able to see that they can not only live, but live with purpose and values. Try and imagine what it is like for such a person to live without God, and then try and imagine yourself living such a life.

The second point is to recognize that this reliance on faith—an inner conviction which is not based on reason or evidence but is seen as a source of knowledge—has to be viewed honestly as a risky strategy. What needs to be acknowledged is that around the world people have the same kind of conviction but with very different specific content. As an extreme example, people have felt convinced that God was calling them to commit acts such as the September 11, 2001, attacks on the United States. On a more everyday level, people tend to understand the God they feel the presence of in terms of the image of God presented to them by their local religion. People in Muslim countries, for instance, do not feel the presence of Jesus. Indeed, even within Christian cultures, what people report to know the existence of changes over time and across denomination. Most strikingly, whether people say they feel the presence of God, Jesus, or the Holy Spirit depends a lot on which church they belong to. This is no mere technical issue that can be glossed over by appeal to the doctrine of the trinity—that all three are part of the one God. In the Bible, Jesus often distinguishes himself from God. "Why do you call me good?" he reportedly said. "No one is good—except God alone" (Mark 10:18 and Luke 18:19). This

It's generally not easy to be an atheist in a country where religion inspires fervent passion—and fervent disagreement. However, congressman Pete Stark (D-Calif.) openly acknowledged his atheism on a questionnaire sent to public officials in January of 2007 by the Secular Coalition of America. The American Humanist Association applauded Stark, shown here in 2003, for his stance. He is the highest-ranking elected U.S. official to publicly claim to be an atheist.

shows why the difference between the three members of the trinity is important for Christians, and thus why it should be puzzling that different people feel a direct conviction that one of the three exists.

For many atheists, the mere fact that people use the same grounds—personal conviction—to justify belief in different, incompatible religions is enough to show that such convictions cannot be the proper basis for religious belief. This is because these convictions support all religions equally, yet not all can be true. Anything that can be used to justify numerous incompatible beliefs cannot be a secure ground for belief. Religious people will still probably reply that they simply can't talk for other people—they know what they know and that is that. But relying on

This photograph was taken during a rally by atheists in front of the Ninth Circuit Court in San Francisco on March 24, 2004. The demonstration was an active gesture of support for a California father who challenged the words "under God" in the Pledge of Allegiance on behalf of his daughter. The original 1892 Pledge of Allegiance did not include the words "under God"; they were added in response to the congressional Oakman-Ferguson resolution, which was signed into law by President Eisenhower in June 1954.

one's personal convictions when there is clear evidence that such convictions are not a reliable source of knowledge, since they convince people of radically different, incompatible things, is to say the least risky, if not plain rash. This is why even some theologians talk about the "risk of faith." Faith is indeed a risk because it runs counter to the kinds of reason and evidence that are reliable and relies instead on reasons and evidence of inner convictions that are unreliable. That is why evidence and argument will always favor the atheist, but also why there will still be religious believers nonetheless.

Militant Atheism

Although I have argued that atheism is not necessarily hostile to religion, there are, of course, some atheists who are hostile to religion, and not just to fundamentalist religions, which attract hostility not only from atheists but moderate religious believers. Atheism which is actively hostile to religion I would call militant. To be hostile in this sense requires more than just strong disagreement with religion—it requires something verging on hatred and is characterized by a desire to wipe out all forms of religious belief. Militant atheists tend to make one or both of two claims that moderate atheists do not. The first is that religion is demonstrably false or nonsense, and the second is that it is usually or always harmful.

Consider the charge of falsity first of all. Bearing in mind what I have already argued about faith's need to go beyond, and indeed sometimes ignore, strong forms of evidence and argument, it is perhaps a small step from here to conclude that religion is therefore irrational. The problem in making this charge stick, however, is that the disagreement between believers and atheists is often precisely about the proper limits of rationality and evidence in belief. The believer sees the atheist's refusal to believe in anything that is not established by the ordinary standards of argument and evidence as too narrow. Typically believers will talk of atheists needing to open up their hearts to God or being too arrogant in their belief that their standards of rationality are sufficient for understanding all the mysteries of existence. The upshot of this line of argument is that religion may be irrational by certain standards, but then so much for those standards.

A good example of the clash of these two opposing viewpoints can be seen in one of the better arguments in the philosophy of religion, the

The biblical book of Job is perhaps the most widely known formulation of the problem of evil in religious literature. In it, Satan challenges God regarding his servant Job, claiming that Job only serves God for the blessings and protection he receives. God then allows Satan to plague Job in a number of ways, and Job responds by questioning God. God challenges Job in return with a series of questions of his own, after which Job repents. This engraving, published in 1826, is one of a series created by the English artist William Blake to illustrate the story.

so-called problem of evil. This is an argument against the existence of God as usually understood. The idea is simple. God is supposed to be all-powerful, all-knowing, and all-loving. Yet there is avoidable suffering in the world. When we say avoidable, we do not just mean that it could be avoided if people acted differently. We also mean avoidable in the sense that a creator of the universe could have avoided such suffering ever coming to be. For example, there seems to be no reason why God could not have created a universe where extreme pain and particularly nasty diseases were not possible. He could also have made human minds more robust so that the lack of empathy required to torture other people was not possible.

The existence of avoidable suffering in the world seems to be an undeniable fact. This must mean one of three things: God can't stop it, which means he is not all-powerful; he doesn't want to stop it, so he isn't all-loving; or he doesn't know about it, which means he isn't all-knowing. This is the so-called problem of evil, and it seems to present a strong case for saying that the traditional Judeo-Christian God can't exist.

There is a way out: God can stop it and wants to stop it but doesn't because it is better for us in the long run that such suffering exists. Such attempts to reconcile the existence of evil and God are known as theodicies, and these are further examples of apologetics. But as with all apologetics, the problem is that the arguments serve the needs only of the believer. For many who believe in God, the problem of evil is a problem, not because it genuinely threatens to undermine their belief, but because they want to be able to explain what on the face of it looks inexplicable. But crucially, many religious believers would be prepared to live with the inexplicability of evil if they could not find a decent theodicy. For many believers, the existence of God is like the existence of time—they believe it exists even if its existence seems to generate logical paradoxes.

For the atheist, the problem of evil demands an answer, and an inability to provide a good one adds to the case against God's existence. For the believer, a solution would be nice, but is not necessary. For militant atheists, this is evidence that religious believers have effectively opted out of the usual standards of truth or falsity. Their refusal to be bothered by seeming contradictions shows that they are essentially irrational in their beliefs. Religion is thus by all ordinary standards demonstrably false, and this claim can only be refuted by rejecting the standards of proof and evidence that intelligent discourse relies upon.

I have a great deal of sympathy with this militant view, but am held back from embracing it by a simple methodological principle I described earlier: avoid dogmatism, meaning always leave open the possibility that one is wrong. I think that the arguments all do point toward the falsity of religion. But because there are no standards for judging these questions shared by atheists and believers, I think that simply asserting that one's own standards must be right is dogmatic. It is enough for me that the arguments and evidence, to my mind, all point to the falsity of religion. I also think that all rational people should agree with me on this, but a good deal do not, and I think it healthier to at least admit the possibility that there is something in what they believe than to simply stamp my foot and curse their stupidity. Though, of course, I do that from time to time as well.

Harmful Religion

The second ground for being a more militant atheist is the claim that religion is harmful. One way of making this case is to say that it is always a bad thing to believe what is false and that since religion is false, it is always bad. "Harm" is here something obviously more abstract than physical harm and implies some kind of lack of integrity to the truth.

The problem with this line of attack is that it only justifies hostility to a belief if it is certainly false, since people disagree about many things and were we to be hostile to all of them the world would be a terrible place. So in order to be militant on these grounds, one would also have to be dogmatic in one's atheism, a stance I rejected in the previous section.

Many atheists believe that religion encourages us to seek rewards not in the here and now but rather in the world to come. One of the most well known religious visions of the afterlife occurs in Dante's epic poem *Paradiso* (1308–21). This 1867 engraving by Gustave Doré illustrates canto 31, in which Beatrice and Dante gaze upon God and his throng of angels and saints, who form the shape of a rose.

An alternative line of attack is to follow Nietzsche (accurately or not) and say that religion is always harmful because it is life-denying rather than life-affirming. Religion encourages us to seek rewards in the illusory next world rather than in this one and therefore robs people of the motive to make the most of the only life they have. The problem here is that not all religious belief is actually life-denying. Certainly, religions teach a certain amount of restraint, but so do all ethical systems. And it certainly does seem to be true that many religious believers do lead full and happy lives. So as grounds for taking a militant line against all religion, this seems rather shaky.

A third idea is that one cannot separate out religion's harmful effects from its more benign ones. Certainly, if you turn up at a typical Church of England Sunday morning service you won't find anything too objectionable. But moderate religious belief is part of a network of belief that includes the more harmful fundamentalist wings. It is just an illusion to think that one can exist without the other. Moderate religious belief is part of the justificatory framework that legitimizes more extreme beliefs. Fundamentalism needs moderate religion because without it it would be recognized for the dangerous nonsense it is. I think there is something in this, but I am concerned that the same argument could apply to any belief which comes in moderate and extreme forms. For instance, misogynists attempt to legitimize their beliefs by appealing to evidence that suggests there are differences between men and women and exaggerating the significance of these. But misogyny is not the same as believing in certain sex differences, and to oppose the latter because of its association with the former is to confuse reasonable beliefs with mindless prejudices.

I am not then convinced that a strong case can be made that religion is essentially and especially harmful. Nor do I believe that a firm belief in the falsity of religion is enough to justify militant opposition to it. At root, though, I think my opposition to militant atheism is based on a commitment to the very values that I think inspire atheism: an open-minded commitment to the truth and rational inquiry. These are rightly called values because they express not only claims about what is true but about what we feel to be most important. Hostile opposition to the beliefs of others combined with a dogged conviction of the certainty of one's own beliefs is, I think, antithetical to such values. Reason and argument are not just tools to be used to win over converts. They are processes that need to be engaged with, and to engage in them with other people one needs to be open to their alternative viewpoints. They cannot be engaged with properly if they are seen as battering rams to destroy the edifice of religious belief.

Conclusion

A great atheist read is Bertrand Russell's *Why I Am Not a Christian*. I thoroughly enjoyed reading it, yet felt that if Russell intended the book to speak to Christians, he had entirely failed. In this chapter I hope to have explained why. One can make a strong case against religious belief and one can show how the traditional arguments for religious belief are hollow. One can even explain how belief often rests on personal convictions which are an unreliable source of knowledge. But the problem with using such arguments to persuade others to become atheists is that believers often do not even accept their founding assumptions. They are starting from somewhere else. The atheist may begin with the basic laws of logic, such as the principle that a thing cannot both be and not be at the same time. But the believer often begins with a conviction that God exists that is even stronger than the logician's belief in first principles. This belief trumps all reason.

The best we can do therefore is to show believers who may think that they have rational grounds for their belief that they are wrong. We can force them to choose, in other words, between taking the risk of faith and restricting their use of reason to apologetics, or giving up their religious belief altogether. I think that relatively few will take the second path. But as more do so, and religious convictions become less and less likely to be passed on by parents, educators, and the Church, so the force of reason may generally hold more sway. Religion will recede not by atheists shouting condemnation, but by the quiet voice of reason slowly making itself heard.

SEVEN

Conclusion

•

Another Time, Maybe

IN A SHORT BOOK LIKE THIS it is inevitable that much has been left out. Although I offer no apologies for these omissions, it is worth pointing in the direction of some of the other lines of inquiry about atheism that readers may wish to pursue.

First, I have not spent a lot of time discussing the thoughts of particular great thinkers of the past. This is because I wanted to keep the focus on arguments which have the most general force and appeal rather than the specific words of specific thinkers. For those interested in what the greats have thought, the works of David Hume,

Los Caprichos **is a set of eighty prints** created by the Spanish artist Francisco Goya during the 1790s. Perhaps the best known of the collection is this one, *The Sleep of Reason Produces Monsters*. The prints were Goya's way of condemning the society in which he lived, including its penchant for superstition and the general decline of rationality—qualities that atheists would say characterizes religion in all its forms.

The work of Albert Camus
(1913–60), including the novels
The Plague and *The Stranger*,
resists easy classification.
Camus denied that he was an
existentialist, and took a stance
against surrealism, but yet some
readers identify his first significant
contribution to philosophy as
being his idea of the absurd, which
results from our desire for clarity
and meaning within a world that
offers neither. Camus appears here
in a 1959 photograph.

Friedrich Nietzsche, Sigmund Freud, Bertrand Russell, Jean-Paul Sartre, and Albert Camus are well worth your time. Some suggestions are listed in the reading and references.

Second, I have not discussed some of the more sophisticated defenses of theistic belief, for the simple reason that I did not want this book to be detailed discussion of the failings of religion but a rigorous defense of the strengths of atheism. For those interested in the best religion can now offer, the works of the Christian philosopher Alvin Plantinga are of great interest, as is the nonrealist theology of Don Cupitt. Cupitt finds himself under fire from Christians and atheists, who both think he is actually an atheist after all and should just admit it, but I think his attempt to save something distinctive from the wreckage of religious belief is admirable and has lessons for believers and atheists alike.

Alvin Plantinga (b. 1932) is a professor at the University of Notre Dame who was called "America's leading orthodox Protestant philosopher of God" by *Time* magazine. Plantinga, seen in this 2005 photograph, applies modern analytic philosophy to some of the age-old questions about God and the universe.

Another theme that has not been discussed in detail is the specific nature of the threats science makes to religious belief. I have focused instead on the wider and more positive issue of how rationalism supports atheism. I also think the science versus religion issue is a little tired and has been discussed many times already.

A fourth line of attack against religion, which I have again avoided to keep the emphasis on the positive, involves claims that religious belief is literally nonsensical or incoherent. These kinds of arguments were popular among the logical positivists in the early twentieth century and were brought to the British public's attention by the philosopher A. J. Ayer. However, logical positivism's star has faded and I am unconvinced that the best way to engage with religious believers is to start from the premise that their beliefs are gibberish, rather than just false.

Humanism

The kind of positive atheism I have been arguing for in this book is sometimes called humanism. In the broad sense of the term, humanists are simply atheists who believe in living purposeful and moral lives. However, I have preferred the more general term "atheist" for several reasons. First of all, humanism is more ambiguous: there are people who call

themselves Christian humanists, for example. Second, "humanist" is not a term most atheists use for self-designation. There are a few explanations for this. The first is that, since most developed countries have organized humanist membership associations, some people think that being a humanist is like being a member of a quasi-religious group. So if they are not members of their national humanist association, they are not humanists. I think this is false, but as a matter of sociolog-

The philosopher A. J. Ayer (1910–89), shown here in 1974, was a professor of logic at Oxford University and one of England's leading humanists.

ical fact, the existence of humanist groups does have the consequence that they have become the main point of identity for people calling themselves humanists.

Another reason why people might avoid the term is that there is a more particular kind of humanism which is a very specific subset of atheism. This kind of humanism focuses on the "human" part of the word and is founded on the idea of the superiority of the human race and the desire to celebrate and further the good of the species. Many atheists and other types of humanist reject this because they do not see any reason to glorify *homo sapiens* or make the species the central point of our concern. Rather, our concern should be with individual lives, and also perhaps the welfare of other species who are capable of complex consciousness. Within the broad movement of humanism there is an ongoing debate about how much concern we should give to other animals, so it would be wrong to think that all humanists share this anthropocentrism. Nevertheless, because some branches of humanism are species-centric in their concerns, some people are wary about calling themselves humanists.

I don't much care what label we use—for me the terms positive atheist and humanist (with a small h) are coterminous. There is more potential for confusion if we use the term "humanist," but it is certainly worth pointing out that the atheism which has been described in this book really is a form of humanism.

Return to the Dark Side

I started this book talking about the slightly sinister, threatening image atheism has. In many ways, the whole purpose of the book has been to dispel this image. Nevertheless, as we come to the end it needs to be acknowledged that atheism does retain some edge of darkness, but for different reasons.

Many atheists throughout history have compared their belief with a form of growing up. Freud, for instance, saw religious belief as a kind of regression to childhood. With religion, we are like children who still believe that we are protected in the world by benevolent parents who will look after us. It is no coincidence that God is referred to as father in the Judeo-Christian tradition.

Psychoanalyst Sigmund Freud viewed religion, in part, as a regression to the condition of childhood. Said Freud in *The Future of an Illusion* (1927): "The gods retain the threefold task: they must exorcize the terrors of nature, they must reconcile men to the cruelty of Fate, particularly as it is shown in death, and they must compensate them for the sufferings and privations which a civilized life in common has imposed on them." Freud saw religion as an illusion, the fulfillment of "the oldest, strongest, and most urgent wishes of mankind." This photograph of Freud was taken in 1938.

Atheism is the throwing off of childish illusions and acceptance that we have to make our own way in the world. We have no divine parents who always protect us and who are unquestionably good. The world is instead a big and scary place, but also one where there are opportunities to go out and create lives for ourselves.

The loss of childhood innocence is a double-edged sword. There is something to lament and something to fear, hence the dark tinge of an atheist belief system which is akin to this loss. But it is also the precondition for meaningful adult lives. Unless we lose our childhood innocence we cannot become proper adults. In the same way, unless we cast off the innocence of supernatural world views, we cannot live in a way that does justice to our nature as finite mortal creatures. Atheism is about moving on and taking the opportunities that life affords, and that carries with it risks of failure and the rejection of reassuring illusions.

It is this realism that means atheism cannot ever be presented as an undiluted, positive joy. Real life is about accepting ups and downs, the good and the bad, the possibility of failure as well as the ambition to succeed. Atheism speaks to the truth about our human nature because it recognizes all this and does not seek to shield us from the truth by myth and superstition.

REFERENCES AND FURTHER READING

•

WHAT IS ATHEISM?

I avoided reading Daniel Harbour's *An Intelligent Person's Guide to Atheism* (London, Duckworth, 2001) so I wouldn't be writing this book in its shadow. However, I have heard many good things about it and shall be picking it up as soon as I finally put my mouse down.

Gilbert Ryle's idea of the category mistake is extremely useful for understanding the naturalist-physicalist world view. It is described in his *The Concept of Mind* (London, Hutchinson, 1949).

THE CASE FOR ATHEISM

The classic philosophical texts mentioned are all available in various editions: David Hume's *An Enquiry Concerning Human Understanding* (1748), Søren Kierkegaard's *Fear and Trembling* (1843), and Blaise Pascal's *Pensées* (1660). The latter's famous wager argument is widely anthologized and is in Nigel Warburton's *Philosophy: Basic Readings* (London, Routledge, 1999).

A good introduction to the philosophical issues of the self is Jonathan Glover's *I: The Philosophy and Psychology of Personal Identity* (London, Allen Lane, 1988).

For a comprehensive guide to argumentative moves and methods, I'll be brazen and recommend my and Peter S. Fosl's *The (Halic) Philosopher's Toolkit: A Compendium of Philosophical Concepts and Methods* (Oxford, Blackwell, 2002).

ATHEIST ETHICS

Plato (c. 428–347 BCE) presents the Euthyphro dilemma in his dialogue called, surprisingly, *Euthyphro*. Kant discusses his categorical imperative and the universal form of moral law in his *Groundwork of the Metaphysics of Morals* (1785). Aristotle (384–322 BCE) discusses character and human flourishing in his *Nicomachean Ethics* (often just called *Ethics*). Mill advocates his consequentialist philosophy in *Utilitarianism* (1861). Hume talks about reason being the slave of the passions in his *Treatise of Human Nature* (1739–40), but his main work on moral philosophy is *An Enquiry Concerning the Principles of Morals* (1751).

For existentialist moral philosophy, read Sartre's short but sweet *Existentialism and Humanism* (London: Methuen, 1948). The Woody Allen short story is "The Scrolls," found in *Complete Prose* (New York: Random House, 1991).

Finally, an excellent single volume containing short essays on almost every aspect of moral philosophy is *A Companion to Ethics*, edited by Peter Singer (Oxford: Blackwell, 1991).

MEANING AND PURPOSE

The works already cited by Sartre and Aristotle are also relevant to this theme. Nietzsche's *On the Genealogy of Morals* (1887) discusses the idea of slave morality. Not many contemporary moral philosophers tackle the issue of the meaning of life directly. One who has done so is Thomas Nagel, and his *Mortal Questions* (Cambridge University Press, 1979) and *The View from Nowhere* (Oxford University Press, 1986) both have sections devoted to it.

To understand evolution and how it doesn't explain the meaning of life, Richard Dawkins's *The Selfish Gene*, 2nd ed. (Oxford University Press, 1989), remains the classic text.

The Ray Bradbury short story is in his *The Martian Chronicles*, a.k.a. *The Silver Locusts* (London: Rupert Hart-Davis, 1951).

ATHEISM IN HISTORY

There are not many histories of atheism. Fortunately, *Western Atheism: A Short History* by James Thrower (New York: Prometheus Books, 2000) and *A History of Atheism in Britain: From Hobbes to Russell* (London: Routledge, 1988) between them cover most of what you'll want to know.

The Encyclopedia of Politics and Religion, edited by Robert Wuthnow (London: Routledge, 1998), is an excellent source of information about the roles of religion and atheism in history. See especially the entries on "Atheism" by Paul G. Crowley (pp. 48–54), "Fascism" by Roger Griffin (pp. 257–64), "Germany" by Uwe Berndt (pp. 299–302), "Holocaust" by Kristen Renwick Monroe (pp. 334–42), "Italy" by Alberto Melloni (pp. 399–404), "Papacy" by R. Scott Appelby (pp. 590–5), "Russia" by Michael Bordeaux (pp. 655–8), and "Spain" by William Callahan (pp. 711–14).

Emilio Gentile's discussion of the sacralization of politics is in *Le religioni della politica. Fra democrazie e totalitarismi* (Roma Bari: Laterza, 2001).

Truth and Truthfulness by Bernard Williams (Princeton: Princeton University Press, 2002) contains an interesting discussion of Thucydides and the study of history.

AGAINST RELIGION?

Interviews with Russell Stannard and Peter Vardy in which they talk about what grounds their religious faith are found in *What Philosophers Think*, edited by myself and Jeremy Stangroom (London: Continuum, 2003).

Two very different introductions to the philosophy of religion are *Arguing for Atheism* by Robin le Poidevin (London: Routledge, 1996), which takes a fictionalist line, and the more traditionally neutral *God of Philosophy* by Roy Jackson (Sutton: TPM, 2001).

Anyone still impressed by the argument from design should read Richard

Dawkins's *The Blind Watchmaker* (New York: W. W. Norton, 1986). Hume's *Dialogues Concerning Natural Religion* (1779) still stand up well as devastating attacks on traditional arguments for the existence of God.

Finally, *Why I Am Not a Christian* by Bertrand Russell (London: George Allen and Unwin, 1957) is a great read for atheists and agnostics, but unlikely to sway the committed.

CONCLUSION

Some classic texts by the greats are the *Myth of Sisyphus* by Albert Camus (London: Hamish Hamilton, 1955), *The Future of an Illusion* by Sigmund Freud (London: Hogarth Press, 1928), and *Language, Truth, and Logic* by A. J. Ayer (London: Victor Gollancz, 1936).

For a look at how science challenges many of our long-standing beliefs, try Daniel C. Dennett's *Darwin's Dangerous Idea* (New York: Simon & Schuster, 1995).

Don Cupitt has written many books on his nonrealist theology. *The Sea of Faith*, 2nd ed. (London: SCM Press, 1994), is recommended. For Plantinga's sophisticated Christian thought, a good place to start is *The Analytic Theist: An Alvin Plantinga Reader*, edited by James F. Sennett (Michigan: Eerdmans Publishing, 1998).

INDEX

•

Page numbers in *italics* include illustrations and photographs/captions.

PICTURE CREDITS

•

Mundas-et-Infans-frontispiece-1522.png/User: DionysosProteus; 74: Starved girl.jpg/Author: Dr. Lyle Conrad; 77: Kant foto.jpg/User: Tenzintrepp; 88: Friedrich Nietzsche drawn by Hans Olde.jpg/User: Berteun; 89: Evolution on a wall.jpg/Author: Paul Keller; 90: Maslow's hierarchy of needs.png/Author: J. Finkelstein; 91: Goals affirmation poster, Navy · DF-SD-04-09850.JPEG/ Author: Mitch Fuqua; 98: Carcassonne cadran solaire.jpg/Author: fdecomite; 101: Z The End Notorious.png/User: Edgar Allan Poe; 106: Prague land-scape 18805.jpg/Author: pcarboni; 108: Parlament Vienna June 2006 184. jpg/Author: Gryffindor; 111: Thales in Nuremberg Chronicle LIXr.jpg/User: Tomisti/Source: http://www.beloit.edu/~nuremberg/book/images/People/ Classical/Philosophers/big/Thales%20LIXr.jpg; 117: Déclaration des droits de l'homme et du citoyen 0613.jpg/User: Rama; 120: DSC03075.JPG/User: Bigjoe5216; 122: Cellarius ptolemaic system.jpg/User: Rivi/ Source: http:// nla.gov.au/nla.map-nk10241; 123: Francisco Franco Official Portrait.jpg; 124: HitlerMussolini1934Venice.jpg/User: Madmax32/Source: Istituto Nazionale Luce/Library of Congress; 127: Stroop Report - Warsaw Ghetto Uprising 06.jpg/Author: Unknown Stroop Report Photographer/User: Jarekt; 129: Cult of stalinality.jpg/User: Anynobody; 132: Perm-36-5.JPG/Author; Wulfstan; 139: Carlo Crivelli 007.jpg/Source: The Yorck Project: *10.000 Meisterwerke der Malerei.* DVD-ROM, 2002. ISBN 3936122202. Distributed by DIRECT-MEDIA Publishing GmbH; 140: UniverseEvolution WMAP mudo.jpg/ Author: Luis Fernández García/Source: NASA: Theophilus Britt Griswold – WMAP Science Team; 143: Schnorr von Carolsfeld Bibel in Bildern 1860 004. png/Source: McLeod; 151: William Blake 007.jpg/Source: The Yorck Project: *10.000 Meisterwerke der Malerei.* DVD-ROM, 2002. ISBN 3936122202. Distributed by DIRECTMEDIA Publishing GmbH; 154: Paradiso Canto 31.jpg/User: Wikibob/Source: http://dore.artpassions.net

BRIEF INSIGHTS

•

A series of concise, engrossing, and enlightening books that explore
every subject under the sun with unique insight.

Available now:

THE AMERICAN PRESIDENCY
Charles O. Jones

JUDAISM
Norman Solomon

ATHEISM
Julian Baggini

LITERARY THEORY
Jonathan Culler

BUDDHISM
Damien Keown

MODERN CHINA
Rana Mitter

THE CRUSADES
Christopher Tyerman

PAUL
E. P. Sanders

EXISTENTIALISM
Thomas Flynn

PHILOSOPHY
Edward Craig

HISTORY
John H. Arnold

PLATO
Julia Annas

· · · · ·